MW00650382

A Rainbow Book

Lies, Damned Lies, and Testimony

Tell It to the Magistrate!

JOHN JASPER

RAINBOW BOOKS, INC. • FLORIDA

Library of Congress Cataloging-In-Publication Data

Jasper, John. 1946-
  Lies, damned lies, and testimony : tell it to the magistrate!
  / John Jasper.
    p.   cm.
  ISBN 1-56825-069-X (alk. paper)
    1. Law--United States--Anecdotes. 2. Criminal justice,
Administration of--United States. 3. Magistrates--
Virginia--Anecdotes. 4. Jasper, John, 1946-   . I. Title.
K184.J37 1998
345.73'o5'092--dc21   97-41223
                                                             CIP

Lies, Damned Lies, and Testimony: Tell It to the Magistrate!
© 1999 by John Jasper

Publisher
    Rainbow Books, Inc.
    P. O. Box 430
    Highland City, FL 33846-0430

Editorial Offices and Wholesale/Distributor/Retail orders:
    Telephone: (888) 613-BOOK (orders only)
    Telephone/Facsimile: (941) 648-4420
    Email: RBIbooks@aol.com

Individual/Retail Orders:
    Telephone: (800) 356-9315
    Fax: (800) 242-0036
    Online from (http://www.) upperaccess.com, amazon.com,
        and barnesandnoble.com

All events depicted are factual. For clarity and continuity, some changes in context were necessary. Names have been changed to protect the rights and privacy of all persons.

Manufactured in the United States of America.

To Christine.

My sincerest thanks to Ann Webster for her help, humor and patience. Thanks also to Jim Jasper for his invaluable suggestions. And to my brother Jerry, a classy guy, thank you for putting up with me.

Contents

Chapter 1

Help Wanted

MAGISTRATE — Shift work; evening, weekend, and holiday hours required. Serves as judicial officer at various police stations. Apply Room 102, Adult Detention Center.

*T*hat's an ad you don't see in the help wanted columns every day. But there it was, alphabetically between laborers and maids. A very curious ad indeed. Advertising for a judge in the newspaper?

I mulled it over for a while and reread the ad a few more times. I was intrigued, but I was also a little suspicious. In the back of my mind was the thought that there was a scam occurring in room 102. Then it was the Adult Detention Center, so it had to be legitimate, didn't it? There was only one sure way to find out. So off I went, seeking room 102. The worst that could happen was that I would be the victim of some sort of practical joke and laughed right out of the place. The thought almost turned me back, but my curiosity won out and I kept on. Such moments change people's lives.

I walked into the visiting area of what had been known in the county for the last two centuries as the jail. In these more politically correct times it is the "Adult Detention Center". Apparently, the jailors — probably known now as "attendants" or some such — were either unaware of the new, friendlier image or were just mad as hell about it. My reception was downright intimidating.

"Excuse me, could you direct me to room 102?"

"No!" snorted the jailor at the desk, his heavy jowls cutting the word short.

I had encountered friendlier Pit Bulls.

"Thank you."

Perhaps this other jailor over here — the one reading a newspaper. He *seemed* less threatening.

"Excuse me, could . . ."

"It ain't visiting hours."

Definitely a little frosty around here. Maybe this is just a bad idea, and I should go home before I get hurt. Oh, well. There's one more deputy — what the hell — *one* more time.

"Do you know anything about a magistrate job?" I asked, quietly and politely, being very careful not to set off another jailor.

"Nah, but their office is downstairs," he answered, not even looking my way.

Well, that was progress, at least. Before I could

ask how to get downstairs, I found myself alone as the jailors disappeared behind a massive steel door. Not knowing what else to do, I found a less forbidding-looking door and opened it. Unless the magistrate's office was equipped with urinals, this was not the door I sought.

Door number two yielded more promising results. The aroma was not exactly inviting; however, it was somewhat better than the previous door, and there were stairs leading down. With some trepidation, I began to descend.

"And, after all, what is a lie?
'Tis but the truth in masquerade."
— Lord Byron

Chapter 2

Drunk in Public

I was jolted from my reverie by an insistent voice asking, "Sir, will you be writing a warrant?" My eyes slowly refocused on the stern, young state trooper standing before me.

State troopers, God love 'em, give the most boring testimony on the face of the planet. Accurate, all inclusive, detailed — oh, yes. My attention had drifted away as to precisely what numbers this drunk missed in counting backwards from one hundred to eighty or which letters of the alphabet he'd missed or if he'd stuck his finger in his ear instead of on the tip of his nose (with head tilted back and eyes closed, sir).

Discovered by the trooper on the side of the road, and surrounded by twelve empty beer bottles, it had taken several minutes to awaken the drunk. Only then could the trooper determine if those twelve beers had been too much and thus make an arrest for being drunk in public. Troopers are meticulous. Mildly embarrassed about my wandering interest, I wrote the warrant, committed the drunk to jail, and wearily looked at my watch — 3:00 a.m. The ad had read, ". . . shift work required."

In front of me, several officers were waiting to approach (as they say). I peeked at my watch again — 3:02 a.m. Time flies when you're having fun. I looked over at my colleague, also hearing testimony. She saw me out of the corner of her eye and gave me the finger. I flung an imaginary booger at her and called out, "Next case!"

A gigantic county police officer came forward carrying under one arm a minuscule woman, trussed hand and foot, screaming, "Let go of me, you motherf--ker! This ain't no way to treat a lady. I'll sue your miserable ass, you piece-of-s--t cop!"

"Good evening, Officer Smith. I see you've been unlucky enough to come across Miss Jackson in your rounds."

"Yes, your honor," he replied wearily.

"And do you swear that your testimony will be the truth?"

"Yes, your honor."

"Please do proceed."

"Your honor, Miss Jackson was once again at the corner of Route One and Pleasant Valley Drive, accosting drivers at the traffic light, attempting to turn a trick."

"You lying motherf--ker!"

"Thank you for your remarks, Miss Jackson, but if you could wait until the officer finishes his testimony, then I'll listen to you."

"Up yours!"

"Your honor, Miss Jackson appeared intoxicated and since two cars almost ran over her, I arrested her for her own protection."

"Now you're a double-lying motherf--ker!"

"The court duly notes your comments, Miss Jackson."

"Kiss my ass!"

My colleague slipped me a note, "I still say she's your sister, and you just won't admit it."

I slipped a note back to her, "I, too, note a family resemblance — to you. Perhaps it's because she's upside down and not wearing any underpants."

The finger again.

We labored on 'til morning.

"No, no!" said the Queen.
Sentence first, verdict afterwards."
— Lewis Carroll,
Alice's Adventures in Wonderland

Chapter 3

Billy and Barnyard

*T*welve years ago I had descended the stairs to the magistrate's office and discovered, wonder of wonders, that the ad was legitimate and required by state law. I was, after a very bizarre vetting process, duly appointed a magistrate and handed a very thick, loose-leaf binder, which would have been appropriately titled *How to be a Magistrate* — if it had been accurately labeled.

My total legal experience included a stint as a company legal clerk in an Army combat engineer battalion. I had managed to be incompetent enough to allow several completely decent draftees to slip away and be honorably discharged instead of busted in rank for minor, failure-to-do-right offenses. My paperwork had always been praised for its accuracy and detail; however, the fact that the subject soldier frequently had returned to the States and been discharged by the time the Article 15 papers were ready for presentation was problematic. I was chastised a few times, but because of an unassuming manner, no suspicion ever came my way. I have digressed. Back to the subject.

When I inquired about a magistrate's job listed in the newspaper, I was quite unexpectedly ushered into the office of the Chief Magistrate. There I stood, somewhat flustered, in my blue jeans and flannel shirt, being introduced to a severe-looking older man, nattily dressed and wearing a bow tie.

"Chief," my escort said, "this gentleman is responding to the ad in the paper."

The Chief stayed seated behind his desk and stared at me.

His first words to me were not, "Hello," or, "Nice to meet you," but "You married?" Not in a kindly voice, either.

"Yes, sir." Why did this feel like being in the principal's office — again?

"Your wife know you're here?" Gruff voice.

"Uhh — yes, sir." Not sure where this was leading.

"This job has some funny hours. I wouldn't want your wife complaining to me."

"She's not the complaining type, sir."

"Good, fill out this application and bring it back."

The audience was ended. He looked back down at the papers on his desk in obvious dismissal. As I was being shown out by a gentleman who had a friendly, amused smile, I asked, "I didn't get the Chief's name?"

"Oh, it's William DeFoe, but everyone calls him Uncle Billy."

It was the beginning of a tumultuous relationship that occasionally would break out into a guer-
rilla war. No artillery, but plenty of small arms fire.

After returning my application to the chief magistrate and receiving a grump and, "I'll let you know,"
I waited a week with no reply. I had, by this time,
learned a great deal more about magistrates. They
are judicial officers who set bail and issue or deny
arrest warrants, search warrants, and mental detentions. They wield a remarkable amount of power,
and I had never before heard of one. Magistrates are
not required to be lawyers, although some are, and
most of their training is on the job. The appointment, initially for four years, is made by the chief
judge of the county circuit court.

The job sounded very interesting, and since I was
at loose ends at the moment — having recently left
the family construction company — I began to call
the chief magistrate every few days. A distinctive
pattern soon developed in our conversations.

"Any decision on my application yet, Mr. DeFoe,"
I would inquire.

"No, Mr. Jasper, but when a decision is made I'll
let you know," was the usual testy reply.

"Perhaps that might be in the next few days, sir?"

"Who knows."

The man was a wealth of information.

Variations of this conversation went on for several weeks. I didn't push too hard, not wanting to
make anyone angry. No future in that, but I couldn't
let it just drop. Incredibly, this farce went on for
three months before, in complete frustration, I de-

cided on a new approach. It was time to call the man who knew the answers.

I have lived in the county for over forty years. When my father brought us out to Virginia from the big city of Washington, DC, I was two and the county was farmland. The drive to Washington was only about an hour, but the cornfields, dairy cows and barns that were everywhere could have been in Iowa. They're long gone. It's subdivisions, shopping malls, and asphalt now. The last cow headed for greener pastures around 1970.

There's still a lot of green today, but it's mostly five-acre lots with large houses, cutesy stables, and temperamental horses ridden by similarly cutesy and temperamental teenage girls. Suburbia is the dominant theme, though. Townhouses, office buildings, apartments, malls, rush hour, and traffic jams predominate. Where once a few thousand lived now several hundred thousand hustle, rush, and elbow each other.

Immigrants are an important part of the population. They came seeking opportunity and have generally found it. Dozens of languages are heard in the halls at school. Very few cultures are not represented. It has become an international, cosmopolitan, vibrant county. We have rich, poor, diplomats, congressmen, drugs, orchestras, and murders. It's now a jumpin', happenin' place.

A lot of the people who lived here when I was growing up are still here. They're just harder to detect amongst the hundreds of thousands. It was to one of these that I turned for my new approach. The recently retired county sheriff visited my father's place a few times over the years to do a little fishing with some success. A six pound, nine ounce large-mouth bass over his fireplace was, perhaps, my access to some information. I gave him a call and got right to the matter.

"Sheriff, I've applied to be a magistrate, and I've had several conversations with Mr. Defoe about my application. At the moment I'm pretty confused."

To which the sheriff replied, in his usual, affable manner, "Uncle Billy up to his games again?"

Not at all sure how to answer that, I just said, "Uh, I don't know, sheriff. I don't know the man. I do know I've been calling him for three months, to no avail. He doesn't say 'no,' he doesn't say 'yes.' He mumbles a lot. He doesn't tell me to quit calling, but he doesn't tell me to call back, either. I don't know if I'm being too persistent, or not persistent enough. I've gotten nothing out of him. Am I too young, too old, overqualified, underqualified, too short, too tall? You see what I mean?"

"Yes, I do. Now, you want this job, do you?"

"Yes, but if it's not to be, I'd at least like to know so I can stop feeling like an idiot calling Mr. Defoe and kissing his butt every few days."

"Don't be too hard on him. He's a Democrat, you know. If you're going to be home for a while, I'll call you back."

No more than ten minutes later, the phone rang.

"Well, you're a magistrate now. I just talked to the chief circuit court judge, Barnyard Billings, and he's making the appointment now. You'll be hearing from Uncle Billy this afternoon."

I was stunned. Three months and all it took was one call to a guy named Barnyard? *Barnyard?* Was that good, or had I just acquired a new boss and sworn enemy at the same time? Many thanks to a certain largemouth bass who gave his all, but I was somewhat apprehensive about the rapid sequence of events that had just occurred. Suddenly, I wasn't looking forward to the call from the chief magistrate who had just been circumvented, however unintentionally, by the son of a friend of an ex-sheriff who liked to fish. And a Republican to boot. Only later did I learn that I was just working the system, and it was the way things were always done. I also learned that Barnyard's real name was Barnhart.

Chapter 4

Everybody's Innocent

I did get the call from Uncle Billy that the sheriff said was forthcoming. He didn't sound happy. I was to learn, in time, that Billy never sounded happy. Billy spent most of his time grumbling, mumbling, and fussing. So much so that every Christmas it became a tradition with me to put a sign on his door that read, "Ebeneezer DeFoe." It was a tradition that Billy never did warm to.

"Be in my office at ten in the morning, and we'll get you sworn in," was the totality of the call. No mention of the ex-sheriff or Barnyard or my three months of calls. I was to learn later that all appointments were made this way. Uncle Billy would never make a decision, and it was only when someone approached the chief judge of the circuit court directly that appointments were made. The good-old-boy system was alive and well, and Billy relied on it heavily.

Anyway, I arrived at ten in the morning and the

deed was done. I was a magistrate of the Commonwealth of Virginia with all the duties and honors at-
tended thereto. But now what? I had been in a court-
room all of once in my life — that being to fight a
speeding ticket (unsuccessfully). I discovered that I
would go to Richmond for a week of training, but
other than that I was completely ignorant of the process that was supposed to turn me into a function-
ing judicial officer.

After the swearing in, I followed Uncle Billy back
down to the magistrate's office to sign some forms.
While I was waiting, I observed some magistrates in
their natural habitat, performing their duties. Words
such as capias, dip, detainer, writ, bailiwick and gra-
vamen were being tossed about. As I watched and listened, a small doubt began in the back of my mind
about my suitability for this job. I saw people in tears
being led off in handcuffs to jail; a woman with a small
baby sitting in an anteroom, both wailing; police, some
looking bored, others looking harried, were everywhere.
Two toddlers screeched in excitement as they ran
around the office playing tag. Where was their
mother? The phone seemed to ring nonstop. It was
pandemonium, and the noise level was overwhelming. The office was small, cramped, dingy, and not
particularly clean, and it seemed like there were fifty
people in it — all talking, gesturing, and crying at
once. It looked like the inmates had taken over the
asylum.

As I continued to watch, I began to detect an
order of sorts being maintained by three magistrates,
although at a frenzied pace at which I marveled. It
was like a beehive or an anthill; first glance saw

only chaos, but closer inspection revealed unsuspected orderliness. Everyone wanted a word with a magistrate: bailiffs, police officers, sheriff's deputies, bondsmen, lawyers, citizens. From out of this melee came one of the magistrates, looking, of all things, very relaxed.

"Billy," he said, "the commonwealth's attorney is on the phone, and he's mad as hell about something some magistrate ordered. He's pretty insistent about talking to you."

As Uncle Billy tended to the phone, the man introduced himself.

"Hi, I'm Doug. You coming on board?" And before I could answer. "Good, good. You can see we're a little understaffed right now."

"Is it always like this?" I'm sure I looked a little dubious.

Doug pondered the scene for a moment, "Daywork can be a real bitch. Court's in session. Every decision handed down means somebody loses, and that means somebody ticked off. This jail's got a thousand people in it, and, amazingly, they're all innocent. Oh, maybe a few of the goofier ones might admit to a very remote possibility of some guilty activity, but that's rare. Makes for a lot of unhappy people, inside and out. Every bitch and gripe in the courthouse gets the same response it seems: 'Tell it to the magistrate.' As you have no doubt noticed, our office is in the basement of the jail. It doesn't get any lower than that, and we all know s--t flows downhill. By the time it gets down here, it's gotten pretty concentrated. Not too many of the people who come to see us are in a happy mood, and we don't often give them much reason to leave feeling any better. Some people call this place 'The Molehole.' When they start cooking breakfast in the jail, you can smell the pancakes. But mostly you smell the mole-asses."

As I pondered that gem, not sure what it meant, Doug sauntered back into the fray. I was impressed.

Uncle Billy was disentangling himself from the phone. As I returned my attention to him, I thought how much he was from the old school. Tall, thin, gray-haired, and a bow tie — he never raised his voice. The office had no computers, and the phones were the rotary-dial type. But even those looked too modern around the chief magistrate. It was easy to visualize him in a green-visored accountant's cap with a 1920s style, two-piece telephone on his desk. He tended to mumble and was always difficult for me to hear. His voice was deep and made me think of distant, muttering thunder on a hot summer night.

He seemed to be completely oblivious to the chaos around us. He rummaged around the office some more, having given up on or forgotten about the forms I was to sign. Instead, he came up with a huge, gray, loose-leaf binder titled, in dull red letters, *Magistrate Manual*. He stared at me intently as he ceremoniously handed it to me, growling, "You have to know everything in here. Be back in the morning at eight o'clock. You better be a fast learner."

Chapter 5

Everybody Lies

*7*he next morning I arrived at 8:00 with a certain amount of apprehension. I introduced myself to the two magistrates on duty. It was quiet. No kids, no cops, no crying. I settled myself in a corner and continued with my "How to Be A Magistrate" book. Soon enough, the tempo began to quicken.

First in was a citizen seeking an arrest warrant. Ignorant as I was, I had not known until then that John Q. Citizen could get another citizen arrested. If he convinces the magistrate that he is the victim of a crime committed by another citizen, the magistrate issues a warrant and sets a court date. Both people then show up before a judge and plead their case.

I watched the magistrate put this man under oath and then ask him a series of questions. It involved an assault, as many citizen warrants do. Eventually, the magistrate was convinced that, indeed, an assault had occurred, and he issued a warrant. I was somewhat uneasy about the process and said to the magistrate after the man had left, "You've heard only one side of the story. How can you be sure that man is telling the truth?"

He looked at me tolerantly, thought a second, and said, "I've been doing this for ten years, and before that I was a cop for twenty years. I've been around the block a few times. The one thing that I've learned is that everybody lies. It should be on the wall as a reminder, in large red letters. What we're determining here is how *bad* are they lying. Nobody tells the complete truth. Hell, if everybody told the truth, you wouldn't even need magistrates, judges or juries. Right? In this case, I think the other guy threw the first punch. This guy would have you believe he's as pure as a Christmas snow. What he did was keep running his mouth and generally acting like an a--hole. The other guy had enough and decked him. I think this guy here is probably a real jerk. But there's no law against *being* a jerk. There is one against *hitting* a jerk. You get the idea?"

"I'm learning as fast as I can. Are you saying that man just perjured himself?"

"Probably. And the last twenty people before him who told me their tales of woe probably perjured themselves, too."

"Doesn't anything happen to them?"

"No."

I must have looked a little surprised because he put his hand on my shoulder and said, "Look, if we prosecuted every person who ever told a lie under oath to a magistrate, we'd have to hire an extra judge just to hear those cases alone, and we'd spend hours in court, every day, testifying. Everybody lies, and everybody knows it. The magistrate's job is to figure out what happened, not who's telling the truth. Since everybody's lying, then nobody's telling the truth, so determining what actually happened is what's important. I doubt that makes sense to you now, but it will later. It's too bad we've come to that. Used to be it wasn't that way. But times have changed and not for the better."

"Well, thanks for the insight."

"Any time. It's your first day; I hope you've got a lot of questions."

"I don't know enough to even know what the questions are yet."

"That's why you're here. The more you do, the more questions you have."

During our conversation, Richard, one of the magistrates in the middle of yesterday's tempest came in. Tall, slender, and soft-spoken, he was Billy's assistant. He moved slowly and spoke slowly but had a first-rate legal mind. Not once in all the years I worked with Richard was there a time that he didn't know the answer to a question on law and procedure or wasn't able to research it in minutes. He'd grown up in coal country, dirt poor, but anxious to get out. He'd studied Latin, the classics, and political science. Not able to afford college, he'd come on the county sheriff's department and eventually won a transfer to the magistrate's office. He would one day become chief magistrate.

Richard wore many hats in that office. Perhaps his most trying one was keeping Billy (as in goat) on an even keel. Before being appointed chief in the dim past, Billy had owned a hardware store. He had never changed his ways and was still trying to run the magistrate's office as if it were a country store. As his "employees," we were under constant surveillance.

Billy was always on the lookout for wicked waste. For instance, no legal pads for us. Billy tore up used notes from county board of supervisors meetings; ten to a pack, precisely stapled in the upper left-hand corner. They were printed on one side, we wrote on the other. Ball-point pens? Bring your own! He kept the staples and paper clips locked in his file cabinet. Don't show up for your shift sooner than twenty minutes before the hour or later than fifteen before the hour. If Uncle Billy could have done it, he would have had a time clock by the door. Sometimes it seemed he trusted the inmates more then the magistrates. It was very bizarre to spend the day considering matters involving murder, robbery, search warrants, and such and then have Billy chastise you for not using up one whole side of a note paper before discarding it.

Richard was our voice of reason. He was infinitely patient, sometimes spending hours over several days trying to steer Billy in the right direction. Richard was also known as the "Georgia Mule" for his plodding persistence. When his mind was made up on something, he was not going to stop until he got to the end of the row. It was always an interesting sideplay watching the Billy Goat and the Georgia Mule testing each other's will and endurance. Richard was our advocate and spent a great deal of time trying to convince Billy that we weren't all escapees from Father Flanagan's Boys' Town.

It had fallen to Richard to see if I was trainable. The method was remarkably similar to how I had learned to swim in summer camp — they threw me off the dock into deep water. Richard contended that anyone could read law books and know the law. Look at how many lawyers there were in the country. Using common sense was what mattered, and you either had that or you didn't. Magistrates were paid to think on their feet. Hear the case, make the decision and move on. One doesn't have the luxury of time to consider every possible nuance. That's for the trial judge. You've got dozens of cases to hear and not much time to hear them. Issue the warrant or deny it, but don't agonize over it. Listen closely and make your decision. At the end of the day go home and recharge your batteries for tomorrow.

It sounded too quick and dirty to me. We were making decisions that could change people's lives. As usual, Richard was right. I came to learn that you could listen *too* much. I also learned that, although many people try to lie, very few are good at it. Richard's advice was very straightforward: If you have to pry and tug to get the story out of someone, what are they hiding? The truth! Don't waste your time trying to get the truth out of a liar. Just deny the warrant they want and say, "Good day." It's an uncomplicated and effective approach.

He spent the morning getting me acquainted with terms: DIP — drunk in public; FTA — a warrant of arrest for fail to appear in court; CAPIAS — an arrest warrant issued by a judge or magistrate for violating a

court order; MISDEMEANOR — a crime punished by
no more than a year in jail; FELONY — a crime punished by more than a year in prison; BAIL — the
concept of allowing an arrestee the opportunity to
bond out of jail; BOND — a monetary sum that must
be posted to get out of jail if admitted to bail. Richard spent hours going over dozens of such things.
He was patient and thorough, and I hung in there
with him.

At noon he announced, "I think there's hope for
you. Come back after lunch, and we'll find out."

I couldn't tell if that was a compliment or a threat.
I wandered off to the cafeteria by myself. I would always eat by myself — not by choice but by necessity. It
was always too busy for two magistrates to be gone at
the same time. And Billy, true to form, seemed to re-
sent the fact that some of us would be so presumptu-
ous as to actually leave for half an hour and eat food.
He, of course, brought his lunch in a brown-paper sack
and ate in the office. The case load has gotten to be
such today that going out to lunch at all is a fairly
rare occurrence. Lunch is frequently a three-pack of
peanut butter crackers and a Coke, all consumed while
hearing testimony. If Billy were around today, I know
he'd approve.

When I returned, the scene was beginning to look
like the one I had watched the day before; the important difference being that I was about to become part
of the melee. Richard looked up when I came in and
said to a waiting state trooper, "Jasper will help you."

He then nodded to me, "This trooper needs an FTA."

"Trooper, he's a virgin. Be gentle."

With that confidence-instilling remark, I put the

trooper under oath and fumbled my way through my first warrant. Upon completion I took it to Harold for inspection. He eyed it critically, hemmed and hawed, raised his eyebrows at the smiling trooper, and finally concluded, "Well, I guess it'll do, but Oliver Wendell Holmes you ain't."

He handed it to the trooper. Of course, the trooper had to look it over, too, and with much raising of eyebrows and intense study, did compliment me on the spelling of my name. I told him I'd had a lot of practice. The rest of the afternoon, if anybody needed an FTA, I was pointed out as the resident expert.

Late in the afternoon the first drunk of the day was brought in — handcuffed. He looked like he hadn't bathed in months, and he smelled like rotten onions. Richard, having just finished eating, took one look and quickly directed the officer to me with, "Jasper, as of now, you're the DIP expert, too. It's just like an FTA, except write 'drunk in public' instead of 'fail to appear in court.' And see if you can do that some other place than right here, okay?"

Trying to find some position upwind of the drunk, I wrote the warrant. It wasn't pretty but, then, neither was the drunk, and it got him out of there and into jail. Everyone started breathing again.

"Not too bad," said Richard. "You took care of that pretty quickly."

"His aroma made me unwilling to linger too long on the constitutional questions involved there. In addition, I was afraid he was going to throw up on me."

"There have been some near misses in the past."

An occupational hazard that I would be careful not to forget.

Next on the afternoon's agenda was a "driving while intoxicated" case. DWI cases, I discovered soon enough, are the biggest pain in the rear a magistrate has to deal with. The testimony is tedious, long, and boring. There is usually a drawn-out recitation about why the officer noticed this particular car in the first place. Then detailed testimony about sobriety tests, nose-touching, number-counting, line-walking, speech patterns. After a warrant is issued, the magistrate then has to go through a series of questions with the drunk about his arrest record, job history, marital status, community ties, and financial situation. Frequently, the drunk is indignant and combative, determined not to give any information because he feels he shouldn't have been arrested in the first place. Convincing a mean drunk to be reasonable and cooperative is not a particularly rewarding experience.

The robbers, muggers and murderers are infinitely easier to deal with. Most of them have been through the system before, and they know not to buck it. It's easier and quicker for everyone that way. But not the DWI. He, or now all too frequently she, may fume, threaten, demand, pout, and curse throughout the whole proceeding. The DWI who comes before me and just stands there silently, I almost want to kiss.

My first DWI was no exception. He was all of the above and more. While Richard looked on, my probable-cause hearing degenerated into an absurd fiasco.

"Who the f--k is this?" demanded the drunk, as he swaggered up to the counter that separates our office from the holding area. He stared belligerently at me from a foot away.

"That's the magistrate, and I'd watch my mouth if I were you," the cop sternly warned him.

"Big f--kin' deal."

"It will be a big deal if he decides not to let you out of jail."

"I been in better jails than this before."

Having made known his opinion of the imminent proceedings, it seemed it was now my turn. I put the officer under oath, and we were off.

"I was on routine patrol westbound on Route Sixty-Six when I observed this gentleman's car weaving all over the road when—"

"You lie!"

"You'll get your chance to speak, sir," warned the officer.

"I wan' your badge number," slurred the drunk, as he stared, cross-eyed, at the badge from six inches away. "An' the han'cuffs are too tight. Loos'n 'em."

"You'll get them off when we get into the jail."

The drunk looked defiantly at me, belched, and then, startling the hell out of me, began sobbing, "Please make him take the 'cuffs off."

I looked at Richard, who looked at me and said, "He's not your prisoner. He's in the custody of the police."

I looked back at the drunk, and he'd disappeared. I could hear him whining and sniffling, and I leaned over the counter to see him sitting on the floor in a spreading pool of urine. The officer was keeping a wary eye on that as he took a few steps to the right. I looked beseechingly to Richard, again, who pointed out that the officer needed to finish his testimony. Things were not going well. I moved down to the end of the counter where the officer was, and we continued.

"I got this gentleman pulled over and out of his car. His condition was such that I was unable to administer any field sobriety tests."

By now the drunk was rolling around on the floor, blubbering, and moaning. A number of deputies, hearing the ruckus, came by to see what was going on and were standing around with decidedly bored looks on their faces. Nothing new to them, I guess. He was making so much noise that I couldn't hear the officer, and by now I had a large audience watching me. I didn't have a clue as to what to do next as the man began rolling in the mess on the floor. Another look to Richard, who helpfully asked, "Do you have probable cause that this man was driving drunk?"

"Richard, I think he's even too drunk to walk."

"Then I think you have established probable cause, and you can write a warrant."

At that point the drunk began vomiting and choking. Medics, apparently alerted in advance by somebody that there might be a problem, appeared almost immediately, and the drunk disappeared in a sea of brown deputy uniforms and white smocks. The stench was indescribable. How the medics put up with it from inches away, I couldn't fathom. It was nauseating and disgusting, but I was frozen in place, unable to take my eyes from the insane scene. With amazing speed and efficiency, the drunk was cleaned out and propped up on a bench on the opposite wall. Then everyone again looked at me.

Everybody seemed quite calm, even the drunk for a change. It was very quiet. It seemed I was supposed to be doing something now, judging by the way I was the center of everyone's attention. I was flustered, and my brain seemed to have locked up. A warrant, I thought, finally. Yes, write a warrant. That's what I'm supposed to do. I managed to get that accomplished and then, to my horror, they brought this vomit-encrusted, urine-soaked, evil-smelling human wreck up to me. I noticed that everyone had on rubber gloves. Now what? I was at a complete loss, mind blank, reeling from the sight and smell.

At that point Richard took pity on me and stepped up. "Normally, now, you would conduct a bond hearing, asking this gentleman such pertinent questions as may help you determine the risk of his not coming to court. But we haven't talked about bond hearings yet, and I don't believe the accused here will be able to participate in a meaningful way, anyway. Just fill out a commitment to jail card, set bond at five hundred dollars, and we'll talk to him later."

Everyone smiled, even the drunk, who amazingly mumbled, "Thank you," as he was remanded to the custody of the sheriff — which meant led off to jail, thank God.

As I stood there feeling devastated by my performance, the one thought that kept running through my head was why did everybody keep calling that drunken slob a gentleman? I guess, though, you really couldn't call him Mr. Drunken Slob to his face. I have to admit that later in my career, in my more base moments, that's exactly what I did. But not on Day Number One with DWI Number One.

I hadn't expected everything to go right for me. After all, I hadn't been on the job one full day. I knew I didn't know beans. But I didn't like being sledge-hammered right between the eyes with the fact. Nothing like a little public humiliation to accelerate one's learning curve.

I must have looked pretty beaten up. Richard said, "Oh, don't feel so bad. Even Oliver Wendell had an occasional off day. For your very first DWI, you picked a real humdinger. Sorry about that bond-hearing part. I forgot we hadn't touched on that yet."

About then Uncle Billy ambled in, wrinkled his nose, eyed me suspiciously, and looked over the counter as a mop-and-bucket brigade of inmates cleaned up the mess. He peered at me again and grumbled disapprovingly, "A little early for a drunk."

Well, it wasn't my fault.

He then carefully put on his hat and walked out the door. I came to learn that that was vintage Billy — cryptic looks, few words, zero praise. Not that I was expecting any praise, but he didn't have to look irritated with me. A real peach of a guy. However, that's another story. The boss was gone and, with a nod from Richard, I packed up and thankfully left the scene of the crime. Little did I know that things were going to get worse.

Chapter 6

East County Disaster

*O*n my second day as a magistrate, everything seemed complicated, and I wasn't able to contribute much. Not that I had made any difference the day before. I didn't want to dwell on that. Hoping to make myself useful, I took to answering the phone, since it rang all the time.

There is always a magistrate available to the citizens, twenty-four hours a day, seven days a week. The police department takes full advantage of that availability, and many of the more problematic and peculiar calls are directed to us. I think our telephone number is on the wall in six-foot-high numbers at the police communications center. Of course, many of the calls are legitimate references, but some of them seem to be misdirected from the asteroid belt. I have found myself involved in conversations such that, when I got off the phone, I truly did not have any idea what it had been about. I sometimes wondered who had dialed the phone for some of these people. It didn't seem possible they could have mastered it on their own.

Each call, at least initially, has to be given careful attention. Most people are very inarticulate, especially under stress, and you have to give them time to get out their problem. What at first seems a crank call can easily be someone in need of help and in a very desperate situation. A magistrate issues emergency mental detentions for emotionally disturbed people who are considering or attempting suicide or harm to others. We frequently get calls from the relatives of such people who are under tremendous stress and pressure. When the phone rings, you can't just ignore it. Because of that we tend to be very short with people once we determine that their call is not something about which we can do anything. When you have to stop a bond hearing to answer a phone call from some idiot who wants to know what he can do about the CIA conspiracy he has discovered to rob him of his vital juices, the answer is short and not sweet. The time and effort wasted on the telephone is still a problem today. Four different chief magistrates have failed to adequately handle the problem.

It went down as a tedious, wearing day, and I was exhausted when I went home. Learning a new career, and a bizarre one at that, crash-course style was a formidable challenge.

Day Three arrived, and if I had known what it was bringing I would have never, never shown up. It made Day Two a fond memory. When I walked in the door that morning, Uncle Billy said to me, "A magistrate called in sick at the satellite magistrate office over in the east end of the county."

I didn't like Billy's look and asked, "Why are you telling me?"

"We're sending you down there."

"Who'll be working there?"

"Just you."

"But I don't *know* anything."

"Can't be helped, no one else is available."

"But I don't know *anything*," I pleaded.

"It's in the police station, and you have a telephone. If you have a problem, call us. Nothing ever happens there, anyway."

"But *I don't know anything*."

My heart was racing, and my palms were sweaty. I continued my protests even as Billy was explaining how to get there while he literally shoved me out the door. I had a bad, bad feeling about it.

With great misgivings and barely suppressed panic I arrived at the satellite office, walked in, turned on the light, sat down, and waited. If anybody came in for anything, anything at all, I wouldn't know what to do. Hell, when I got to the station I had to ask someone where my office was. I thought about turning the light back off and closing the door. I didn't see how else I was going to survive the day. I felt overwhelmed, and nothing had happened yet.

The first day of basic training for the Army was the last time in my life when I had no idea at all what I was doing. But there were several hundred other guys in the same situation and no one *expected* you to know anything. As a matter of fact, you were expected *not* to know anything, and you got into trouble if you acted like you did know anything. There was a similarity in that I was scared to death then and I was scared to death now. At least in basic I had a drill sergeant who made sure I learned everything I would need to know. I never thought I would miss my drill sergeant.

The office had a front room for prisoners and a rear private room where I now sat. Into the front room came an officer with two rowdies in handcuffs. It was beginning. The officer seemed very nice and introduced herself.

I said, "Could I see you in the back for a moment?"

When we got there I immediately pleaded my case, "Look, I just got appointed day before yesterday, and if you don't tell me what to do, you'll be here all day while I try to figure it out on my own."

For a moment she looked amazed and then her face softened and she smiled, "When I got pregnant and was off for a few months, they changed all the state code numbers, and I didn't know what was going on when I got back. I know exactly how you're feeling. I got a lot of help then, and I was sure thankful for it. Leave it to me."

She sat down, pulled blank warrants from various cubby holes, wrote up the charges, filled out the commitment-to-jail cards, put herself under oath, had me sign in the right places, wished me luck, and took her prisoners off to jail. What a woman! 'Til the day I die I will be indebted to her. The word was passed around the station of my unfortunate situation, so the police came in either with only very simple things that I could muddle through, and they went directly to the main office with anything mildly complicated.

I thought that was quite decent of them. But that still left the citizen inquiries for me to deal with. Every time someone came into the office it was a guaranteed public humiliation. I couldn't help anybody. Some were nice and said they'd come back another time. Some were not so nice and stormed out. Some were real jackasses who demanded I do something — right then. I had to convince them that I was so ignorant that I was incapable of helping them, no matter how pressing or important their problem.

"Sir, you don't understand. It isn't that I don't *want* to help you, I don't know *how* to help you."

"Then why the hell are you here?"

"I'm not sure myself. I got sent under protest."

"I'm a taxpayer. I demand you do something."

"I don't know how to do something — or anything."

"I'm going to write a letter of complaint to your boss."

"He's the one who sent me here."

"This is ridiculous."

"I agree."

I endured eight very long hours of convincing people that I was incompetent and unable to render them any assistance whatsoever. Every moment of that day is etched in my mind. It was excruciating agony; it was torture by a thousand tiny slashes; it was slow death by humiliation.

I could think of only one other time in my life when things had gone so badly. When I was ten years old my best friend, who was an altar boy, convinced me to be the other altar boy one Sunday when his brother was sick. I had never done it before, but it went okay because I just did what he did. He asked me to help again next Sunday, and I foolishly agreed. Next Sunday he didn't show, and I was on my own. I pleaded with the priest not to do this to me, but he would hear none of it. It was my duty to God, Mary, and Jesus. At ten years of age you don't say, "No," to the priest.

It was awful. I rang the bells when I wasn't supposed to and didn't ring them when I was supposed to. I tripped on the hem of my cassock, forgot to get the wine and water, didn't know the Latin responses, stood at the wrongs times, knelt at the wrong times. The priest was reduced to snapping his fingers loudly whenever he wanted me to do something.

I looked out at the congregation at one time and remember my poor mother sitting there feeling my pain and misery every bit as much as I was. Tears rolled down my cheeks more than once during that mass. At least it was over in an hour (perhaps the longest hour ever in my young life), and I did have my mother to dry my tears and comfort me afterward. And I also got the satisfaction of beating the ever-loving hell out of my buddy the next day.

The thought of doing the same to Uncle Billy crossed my mind several times. Although the idea of such an action was wonderfully appealing, it would no doubt be viewed as particularly bad form to assault the chief magistrate. The altarboy fiasco had been bad enough, but it hadn't gone on for eight hours. Then I thought, good God, what if he sends me here again tomorrow! The thought propelled my mind down an evil path. Maybe I could spike his tires or cut his brake lines. I'd even cut *my own* brake lines to avoid another day like today.

When the evening magistrate arrived, he must surely have wondered at the joyful greeting he received from the new guy. I held the door open for him, got him a cup of coffee, and kept inquiring if there was anything else he needed. Pharaoh returning to his palace was not treated with more honor.

"There is no such thing as justice —
in or out of court."
— Clarence Darrow

Chapter 7

T-R-O-U-B-L-E

*B*loodied, but no longer bleeding, too dumb or too stubborn and only slightly recovered from my fiasco of the day before, I returned to the jail for Day Four. I was prepared to do anything short of kicking Billy in the unmentionables to avoid being sent back to the East County Station again. And then again . . .

Fortunately for Billy's jewels and my continued employment, he had no intention of sending me back. Instead, he was sending me for a prolonged stint to the South County office on Route 1.

"That's a twenty-four-hour office, and the magistrate there will do your training. See Mr. Howard there and work with him for the next several days. He's different, so don't take anything he says to you to heart."

Now what was I getting into? I couldn't take many more surprises. I did know about Route 1, though. From Maine to Florida, I think Route 1 is the same — trashed. Our section of Route 1 was no different.

Honky-tonk bars, flea markets, trailer parks, biker hangouts, flop houses, pawn shops, deserted buildings, and vacant, trash-strewn lots make up the Route 1 landscape. It had been that way ever since I could remember. It had a rough-and-tumble reputation then, and it had one now. Barroom brawls, the occasional stabbing or shooting, a murder every so often, were the more-or-less normal weekend fare. In my pre-magistrate days I never went near Route 1.

I pulled up to the police station in which our office was located. A seven-foot-tall chain link fence with barbed wire on top surrounded the place. Looked about right for the neighborhood. Maybe it wasn't quite Fort Apache, the Bronx, but it had what one could call a "businesslike" appearance. I walked in the front door, where I was examined warily by a desk sergeant behind a bulletproof window. Not a word from him, but the body language was loud and clear. (If you ask me a question and bother me I'll rip your damned head off!) I did see a sign with an arrow pointing to a door marked "Magistrate," and I carefully eased past the scowling guardian.

As soon as I got through the door I was accosted with a loud yelling, "Get out! Get out! Wait your turn!"

I stopped dead in my tracks as I stared at a man behind a counter who was agitatedly pointing his finger at me. There was another person standing on my side of the counter looking over his shoulder at me.

"Get out! Get out! I didn't tell you to come in!"

It was as if I were a recruit who had walked into the sergeant major's office, uninvited. Was everybody nuts down here?

"But, Mr. DeFoe sent me down here. He called

and said . . ."

"Put your things in the back office, then," he
ordered, without missing a beat or changing his tone.
"Don't just stand there. Hurry up, man! Then come
out and listen to what I'm saying. Maybe you'll learn
something. I'm sure you didn't learn anything up there
with Billy."

I'd heard the expression "machine-gun-like
speech," but I'd never really had it aimed at me before.
It made me want to duck. Instead, I scurried to the
back office, dropped my briefcase and manual, and
hurried back out front.

". . . I'm going to give you a little bit of old man
advice." He had his eyes locked on the young man at
the counter. "If she's going to treat you that way, the
only way to fight her is with your hat. Take it and run.
There's a lot of fish in the sea. There's a trolley by
every ten minutes. They're *all* pink on the inside. Do
you get my drift son? She ain't worth going to jail over."

"Yes, sir, I see what you mean. Hey, thanks a lot."

"Anytime. Bicycle, have fun, enjoy, go home."

He whirled around, stuck out his hand and fired
in a booming, staccato voice, "Sorry about that. Hi,
I'm Mike Howard, spelled T-R-O-U-B-L-E. So — Billy
sent you down here to learn something."

"Uh . . ."

"It's about time. I heard we had a new man. I told
Billy to send you down here with me. You've been up
there for three days. I hope you haven't been ruined
already. Damn, those people are dumb. Come on let
me show you around."

And then he finally took a breath.

He took me on a whirlwind tour of the lockup,

the detectives section, roll-call room, locker room, sally port, processing room, parking lot, and janitor's closet. He kept a nonstop patter going the whole time. I guess he was sixty, but he had the energy and enthusiasm of a twenty-year-old.

He leaped immediately into educating me about the "real" world of magistrating. He, of course, did *that* with enthusiasm, too. When I asked questions, he pounced on them with answers. When I didn't have questions, he did. Whenever the police brought in a prisoner, he had me handle it while he hovered six inches off my shoulder. If I started to go astray, he'd jab me in the side with his finger. If he caught me really going off the rails, he'd stop me and, in front of everybody, say, "Don't be stupid. Think. Use your God-given brains, son!"

I suppose some people would have been insulted by him. I learned later that many were. But his enthusiasm, his obvious concern, and his complete openness I found appealing. Once I adjusted to his directness and bluntness, we hit it off fine. If I screwed up, he told me so in no uncertain terms. But he always pointed out how not to screw up that way again. In a court system that I discovered to be ego city top to bottom, in a bureaucracy that was vicious, backbiting, self-indulgent and all too frequently peopled by incompetents, Mike was a jewel. He actually cared about people.

He had been a magistrate a long time; maybe back when Marbury sued Madison. In a system that did not care about people, he was unique. He still cared, and because he cared, he was frequently scorned. Since he was different, he was often ridi-

culed. It didn't bother Mike in the least. He had managed, at one time or another, to outrage almost everyone in the court system, and I think he was secretly a little proud of that. He wasn't always right
in some of his battles with the bureaucracy, but he
always jousted with enthusiasm. I also came to like
Mike because he had a screw loose here and there.

One of Mike's oddball mannerisms was a pen-
chant to use a number of hackneyed expressions he
had been abusing people with for years. They were
just awful, and Mike reveled in them. If you were
wondering a few paragraphs back what Mike meant
when he said, "Bicycle," to the young man he was
giving advice to about his girl friend — to Mike that
meant goodbye. In all the years I knew Mike, I never
one time heard him say marijuana; to him it was
always "wacky-baccy." He had hundreds of such expressions, and I used to plead with him to get some
new writers. Most of his expressions were amusing
the first few times you heard them. But I had to hear
them hundreds of times. The more pained I looked,
the more inspired Mike got:

"We take the long green with the short future, in
God we trust, all others pay cash."

That was Mike's way of saying we took only cash
for bail bonds.

"Uniformed attendants at my hotel."

Translation: jailors.

"Be like MacArthur."

Translation: Come back.

"Got your round heels on?"

Translation: Look out, you're about to get screwed.

Enough of Mike's expressions. You can digest but

so many at once. Back to the subject at hand — my training. I spent a number of weeks with Mike. I wouldn't say he was a patient teacher. He was more like relentless. From the moment I walked in the door until his last lecture at shift's end, usually in the parking lot on the way to my car, he was at me with questions, scenarios, and previous cases. If he thought my thinking on a subject was lazy, he would be hurt. If he thought a question was stupid, he would say so, usually by remarking, "That's the stupidest question I ever heard." You could never accuse Mike of subtlety.

I discovered that I responded to his approach. Being a magistrate, I was quickly learning, is a rough-and-tumble job, and Mike's approach to teaching it was the same. You train a boxer in the ring and give him a few bloody noses in the process. You don't teach him etiquette. You try to knock him out. To be a magistrate, you have to be able to think quickly, on your feet. That's what Mike demanded of me.

When I did or said something stupid, I suffered the consequences: an immediate reprimand and a scolding, usually in front of an audience. He wasn't vindictive about it. He just believed you learned more quickly that way. With me he was right. He was at me hammer and tongs, constantly challenging me. I had to respond. It was either learn or give it up and leave. No doubt if Mike had been a public school teacher in today's environment, he would have been burned at the stake — and it would have been the students' loss.

Chapter 8

Route #1

The standard Route 1 clientele were generally a pretty sorry bunch. On some Saturday nights, when the eight cells in the lockup were full, the total tooth count could be distressingly low. There were also two cells for women, but their occupants often didn't add significantly to the dental number. Those people, not in the cells, coming to seek help from the magistrate were also a pretty downtrodden lot.

Their afflictions are legion; but all too often alcohol and drunkenness were at the root of their multitude of problems. Occasionally, I have been in discussions about the legalization of drugs. I have my doubts. I have dealt directly with the tragedy of alcoholism and its destruction of people, families, children, and lives for years. After listening to hundreds of battered wives and abused children of alcoholics who have given up any hope of a normal life, I do not think we need more legal drugs. The ones that we have are overwhelming us.

Alcoholism is a relentless destroyer. It destroys hope, initiative, honor, dignity, honesty, and loyalty. Work is definitely the curse of the drinking man, as is responsibility. Abuse of alcohol is an epidemic not truly recognized. Oh, it's a topic of discussion, but as a society we tolerate it, even joke about it. The heroin user or the crack addict is never a source of humor — the drunk is.

And it is the wives, husbands, children, and relatives of the alcoholic who suffer most. They have to worry about the beatings and abuse while attempting to carry on some semblance of a normal life. They have to go to work, go to school, pay the bills, and suffer the indignities inherent in such a hardscrabble existence.

The alcoholic stays drunk, anesthetized from the daily struggle of making ends meet and staying alive. Need another drink? Got no money? Beat the old lady until she coughs up the rent money. Or beat her if she's used it to pay the rent. Steal the kids' piggy bank and beat them too if they cry. No humor there that I can see.

There have been weekends when I have written dozens of arrest warrants, and every single one was alcohol related: murder, assault, driving while intoxicated, drunk in public, manslaughter, disorderly conduct — all involving alcohol. And, sadly, women seem to be catching up to men as alcohol abusers at an alarming rate. My hardest moments almost always involve children of alcoholic parents. To see a six-year-old boy trying manfully to comfort his four-year-old sister as the cops try to stop a drunken brawl between their parents is too much to bear.

Legalize drugs? As I said, not until we figure out how to deal with the ones we already allow.

One night, the police brought in a woman they had arrested for reckless driving. The officer had been sitting at a red light when a car skidded sideways through the intersection and then accelerated down the road at high speed, weaving in and out of traffic. There were several near collisions. The officer got the car pulled over before a major accident could occur. What he found was a woman in her thirties who, though not quite legally drunk, had obviously been drinking. Sitting next to her on the front seat was a cute, blue-eyed, blond, seven-year-old little girl licking an ice-cream cone. Her mother, unfortunately, developed quite an attitude with the officer when it was discovered she was driving on a suspended license. She therefore ended up in front of me. The officer was not happy with her.

"Sir, Miss Lancaster here was driving like a maniac in some pretty heavy traffic. When I asked her why she was driving like that she said her daughter had cut herself and she was trying to get to the hospital."

Miss Lancaster gave me a radiant smile and giggled, "That's true."

She just about curtsied as she said it. Something weird going on here.

"Only problem was," the officer continued, "her little girl was just sitting there happily licking her ice-cream cone. That and the fact that the hospital is the other way."

Miss Lancaster bestowed me with another beaming smile.

The officer continued. "I put Miss Lancaster in the back of my cruiser and asked the little girl if she had hurt herself. She looked at me kind of puzzled-like and said, 'No.'"

Miss Lancaster's big smile suddenly disappeared upon hearing that, and she said testily, "She's lying."

"You mean your seven-year-old daughter?" I asked, somewhat taken aback.

"Yes, she knows perfectly well she had a cut lip that was bleeding." Mom was getting real earnest.

The cop said, "That's what she told me, too, your honor. The little girl had a fever blister on her lip, but it wasn't bleeding or anything. I asked her where they were going and she said, 'Home.'"

Mom looked sharply at the cop. "Did she say that? That was really a lie."

"Where's the daughter now?" I asked.

"We were able to get her grandparents to come and get her. They lived just around the corner. I didn't get to talk to them very long, but apparently this is not an unusual occurrence. Miss Lancaster here got pretty agitated when they showed up. It seems they're beginning custody proceedings because of this kind of stuff going on."

I looked at mom and asked, "Is it really worth trying to beat a reckless driving ticket by calling your own little girl a liar?"

No more radiant smiles for me.

The officer added, "You might like to know, your honor, that she has prior drug offenses."

"It would seem with permanent brain damage, too." I looked at her again. "Do you really want to keep saying that your own little girl is a liar?"

She stared at me and with hardness in her voice said, "You don't know her like I do."

The cop just shook his head in sadness. Drugs and alcohol — what a wonderful world!

When Route 1 denizens come to see a magistrate for help, you can be sure they have a bad situation. There is a deep and long mistrust of the police and any authority figures. The magistrate and the courts are somewhere down below root canals and land-lords in their list of things to avoid. To come to the magistrate is putting your head in the lion's mouth. When they do show up, they are either tenuous and hesitant or loud and demanding.

The first type can be, ironically, much more diffi-cult to handle than the second. Loud and demanding is actually pretty easy. You tell them to quiet down and shut up or they'll get tossed out the door — pe-riod. As the magistrate, you have all the high cards. Play by my rules or you don't get to play at all. No compromises, no "Let's make a deal," no haggling. I can help you, but only if I do it my way. End of discus-sion. The blowhard generally settles right down and is usually apologetic. From then on it is simply listen-ing to the complaint and deciding the best solution. It's not very complicated.

With the tenuous and hesitant, you have to com-pletely change your approach and demeanor. They are there for help but are too nervous and afraid to actually ask for it right out. You have to be patient and, hopefully, appear understanding. But you have to appear firm also. You are probably the last hope that they will be able to get help from the court. They want to believe they're doing the right thing and it's important to encourage that. Since you are the court, you'd better be able to instill some confidence and project some authority. If the magistrate appears tenuous and confused, the citizen begins to wonder if this is the thing to be doing. Above all else, you have to listen. The meek will tell you their whole problem but won't have a clue as to what to do about it. Then you have to probe to find out what they're willing to do. Sometimes you find out the answer is not a thing. Those thank you for listening, say they'll think about your suggestions and leave, never to return. Others grab hold of the options you can offer like a drowning person to a life preserver. Those are the most satisfying. You're able to give real help and offer hope. It may be a women's shelter, a mental-detention order, a protective order against an abusing spouse, or an arrest warrant. Whatever it is, it's no doubt an improvement over their present mess and a first and important step in the right direction.

At other times the experience is far from satisfying. Those people who have spent years digging themselves into a deep pit of contradictions, denials, and self deceptions, tend to be the ones who demand instant solutions from you. When you can't offer them that, it is great indignation and, frequently, rage that are hurled at you. Such a woman stormed into the office one night, demanding action against her husband. We pick up the scene in progress.

". . . and I want that miserable bastard out of the house — immediately!"

"How long have you been married?" I asked.

"Fifteen years, that son of a bitch!"

"And tell me again why you're here tonight."

"Because of that slut of his! The miserable son of a bitch has had one slut or another for years."

This was one angry woman.

"And you've known about that all along?"

"Yes."

"And tonight you caught him *in flagrante delicto* in his bedroom?"

"If you mean f--king, not exactly."

"I assume you don't share the same bedroom?" I ventured.

"Like I said, he's been f--king around on me for years."

"And you've tolerated that for years?"

"What could I do?"

"File for divorce," I suggested.

"It wasn't convenient."

I took note of an abundance of diamond-and-gold jewelry.

"But now you feel he's gone beyond the pale, so to speak?"

"He shouldn't bring them right into the house!"

That didn't seem unreasonable.

"So, you've told me you came home and discovered a partially dressed woman in his closet?"

"Yes, and I want his balls for that."

"I don't think there's too much chance of the court ordering that. Why were you looking in his closet?"

"I came home from shopping early, and I heard some noise in his bedroom. I didn't think he was home from work, so I go in there and, son of a bitch, I find them both hiding in the closet."

"And you called the police, and they said, 'Tell it to the magistrate.' What do you want me to do?"

"I want him arrested."

"What charge did you have in mind?"

Slowly and with feeling she replied, "Whatever hurts him the most."

"There is a basic problem," I responded. "I don't hear that any criminal activity has occurred."

"He's screwing another woman, and he's my husband. Isn't that adultery?"

"Yes, that's grounds for divorce, but it's not a criminal act. You don't get arrested for adultery."

"You mean the son of a bitch can get away with this?"

"If you sue for divorce, I imagine it could cost him big bucks, but you've had that option for years, and you haven't done so. You've been looking the other way for a long time. I can't solve the problem tonight with a criminal warrant."

"You mean you're not going to arrest him?"

"That's correct. This is not a criminal matter."

"You suck, and this whole system sucks!"

Variations of the preceding exchange have occurred many times. The magistrate is always the bad guy for not ordering the police to swoop down on the husband with guns drawn and drag him off to jail for thirty days of bread and water, or worse — much worse.

My favorite quintessential Route 1 case began one night with yet another man being brought in for a domestic assault. It seemed to be another garden-variety assault case. Boyfriend and girlfriend get into an argument, and both have been drinking. Boyfriend pops girlfriend, who calls police, and that is why I have gainful employment. In this case, Mr. Lomax, the accused, went with the police quietly enough, which is frequently not the case. Nor did Mr. Lomax cop an attitude with me, either.

"Do you live there with this girl, " I asked.

"Yes, sir."

"Do you have any children together?"

"Yes, sir."

"How many?"

"Three."

"What was the fight about?"

"We was just arguing."

"Anything in particular?"

"It was about her sister."

"What about her sister?"

"Well, sir, she's been out of the house at night a lot lately."

"Why is that a concern of yours, Mr. Lomax?"

"She lives with us."

"Is she over eighteen?" I asked.

"She's twenty-six."

"Why does that concern you then? She's an adult."

"She's got two young kids she should be home with."

"Hmm, I see. So you're sort of looking after the household, is that right?"

"Yes, sir."

"Is she divorced?"

Mr. Lomax began to look a little more uncomfortable than he already was.

"She never was married."

"Oh, you and her sister took her in, then?"

"Um, it's not exactly like that. But she did move in with us."

"Let me get this right. This is your girlfriend's sister, and she has two kids, and they all live with you?"

"Yes, sir."

"Where's the father of her two kids?"

"Umm, they're mine, too, sir."

There was a long silence while I absorbed that.

"I begin to see, Mr. Lomax, how things could get a little testy around your house."

Chapter 9

He's Deaf, I'm Chinese

I continued on with Mike for some weeks and slowly began to get a feel for the job. It would actually be six months before I truly felt comfortable with the position and really thought I knew what I was doing. Before leaving Mike's School of Magistrating, I had what served well as a final-exam event. As Mike said, in his own unique way, after it was over, "If you could straighten out that Chinese laundry fire drill, I guess you can figure out about anything."

For the police, it started badly and immediately went straight downhill. They responded to a 911 call for an assault at a residence. When the two officers arrived, they were met at the door by a young Asian woman with a nasty cut over her eye. She told them her brother had done it, and she wanted him out of the house. When the police entered, they found the brother, who was about twenty years old, quietly studying at the kitchen table. Their mother was apprehensively peeping around the corner. The father, putting on his overcoat, was going out the back door.

He paused long enough to report to the police, "I leave. Everybody crazy here," and disappeared.

The two cops shrugged and asked the young man at the table what the problem was. He looked at them quizzically and then at his sister and also shrugged.

The sister helpfully added, "He's deaf and dumb. He can't speak."

Officer O'Flaherty warily eyed the mother, still peeking around the corner, as he said to the sister, "Why'd he hit you?"

"He should be studying in his room at the dorm, not here. I told him to leave. It's only ten minutes away. I need to study at the table. It has the best light."

"Okay, um, how did you tell him? He's deaf."

"He understands sign language."

Brother had gone back to studying and was ignoring the cops with their guns and mace and billy clubs crowded into the kitchen. Mother had not moved. She kept peering.

Officer O'Flaherty pressed on, "Then what happened?"

"He told me to get f--ked."

"What, in sign language?"

"Of course. So I called him an a--hole."

"In sign language?"

"Yes."

O'Flaherty lost his train of thought wondering what a--hole must look like in sign language.

His partner Officer McDougall took over. "Then what?" It seemed like a good question.

"He hit me over the eye with a ruler."

"Anything more?"

"I called the police."

McDougall and O'Flaherty conferred.

"We'd like to talk to your mother alone."

"You can if you want, but I don't think it will help much."

"Why not?"

"She doesn't speak English."

McDougall and O'Flaherty conferred again. They had their hats pushed far back on their heads now, always a pretty good indication of cop frustration.

"Ma'am, we're going to have to arrest your brother for assault. My partner is going out to the cruiser to get a camera to take a picture of your injury."

Sister suddenly looked panicked. "I don't want him arrested! I just want him to go back to the dorm!"

"Ma'am, you've been assaulted, and you called the police emergency number. He's going to jail. Now stand still while my partner takes your picture. We'll take your brother to the station to see the magistrate about an assault warrant."

"No! Don't! No picture! Don't arrest him." She lunged for the camera as McDougall came through the door.

McDougall, surprised, jerked the camera back hitting himself in the eye with it. O'Flaherty grabbed the sister who was flailing at McDougall and clawing for the camera. Mother finally made her first move of the evening and with screams and shouts launched all 4'10", 85 pounds onto O'Flaherty's back. O'Flaherty probably outweighed the two of them together by 100 pounds, but they both were clawing at him like wildcats. When McDougall tried to pull the mother off

O'Flaherty, the brother jumped McDougall, and the fight was really on. McDougall flipped the emergency call switch on his radio. The brother was jumping around the room using some sort of martial arts, although he seemed to breaking the furniture more than doing any damage to McDougall.

When the cavalry arrived in the form of about ten cops. They saw McDougall and the brother warily circling each other in the living room. McDougall was ready with his can of mace as the black-belt hopeful occasionally broke something while making very weird grunting sounds. O'Flaherty had managed to get the two wildcats off and was attempting to corner them in the kitchen with his billy stick. One would dart from the left and then the other from the right. Each time, McDougall would roar, poke his stick out, and stomp his foot at them. His nose was bloody from the sister popping him with a garlic press. Mother and daughter were screeching, and for a little added confusion, a Pekingese was running around biting any available ankle.

When the ten additional cops hit the door, it was over in a second. Everybody went to jail. The dog was the only exception, and he got locked in the bathroom.

And, thus, the case was presented to me. The sister, who spoke English, was so mad she wouldn't talk. The brother couldn't talk, but the mother who spoke no English wouldn't shut up. Of course, nobody knew what the hell she was saying. Fortunately, there was an officer on duty who knew sign language, which was an amazing stroke of good luck. Everyone took a much-needed cooling off break while we waited for his arrival.

Not that I did nothing while waiting. I spent the time listening to O'Flaherty's and McDougall's testimony. It took me quite a while to sort out who did what to whom how many times. After the officer who could sign arrived, I found myself listening to the officer tell me what the brother had signed to him, which was frequently a translation of what the mother had said to him. Sometimes the sister, who was talking now, would interrupt in English, Chinese, and sign language. O'Flaherty asked the officer what the sign for a--hole looked like.

Eventually, I charged the mother for assaulting McDougall and let her go. They probably didn't have any jail garb for eighty-five pounders anyway. I charged the brother for assaulting the sister and let him go. He did more damage to the furniture than anything else. The sister, who had started this whole thing by calling the police and then wanting to call it off, got charged with assaulting McDougall and O'Flaherty. I held her in the lockup for a few hours until she cooled off, and then I let her brother post her bail. Regrettably, a conflict in my schedule did not allow me to observe the trial. I would have enjoyed watching the judge trying to determine who was guilty of what beyond a reasonable doubt with simultaneous translation in Chinese and sign language.

"Hogans r-right whin he says: 'Justice is blind.' Blind she is, an' deef an' dumb an' has a wooden leg."
— Finley Peter Dunne,
Mr. Dooley

Chapter 10

A Real Cracker Jack Magistrate

Having survived, and even prospered, under Mike's ministrations, I was reassigned to the jail, where for several days I had the remarkable experience of working with the oldest living magistrate in the Commonwealth of Virginia. At least I think he was living. Ferd Hogan seemed older then a moss-covered brick and not much more energetic. Anyone whose first name is Frederick, but who chose to be called Ferd, as in nerd — or worse, can't be too swift of mind. Nor was he particularly dedicated to doing the job at hand. When Ferd decided that he'd done enough for one day, which was never more than what he couldn't manage to avoid, he went home. Sometimes he would tell you he was leaving, sometimes not.

Ferd and I were working a weekend midnight shift together. It was 3:00 a.m., and since the bars close at 2:00 a.m., things were getting pretty busy. Ferd apparently didn't like the tenor of the night so he walked up to me and announced, "I find that I sleep much better if I can get into bed before the sun comes up." Without another word, he walked out the door, leaving me by myself to fend the best I could until the 7:00 a.m. relief arrived. Actually, it never bothered me when Ferd left early. When he was there, you had to work twice as hard correcting everything he screwed up. There were times when he didn't go home that I wished he had. He seemed to be oblivious to all of this, though, and actually thought he was a real cracker jack magistrate.

One day, through what must have been a scheduling error, he was working by himself at a satellite station. An unsupervised Ferd was something difficult to imagine. I answered the phone, and it was Ferd. An officer had brought in a man who was wanted in another state. That required the magistrate to write a fugitive warrant. It's a little complicated, but the average high school senior wouldn't have any problem after being shown how to do one. But here was Ferd, the oldest living magistrate in the universe, on the phone, mystified about a fugitive warrant. Through the eons, he had managed to learn nothing and remember less. Having always worked with someone, he had simply refused to write them because they were a mystery to him. Someone else had always done them.

You might wonder at this time how it was that Ferd was able to keep his job. It's a fair question. There was much speculation around the courthouse on that very topic. I had to conclude that Ferd had photographs of some influential people in bed with young boys or perhaps a farm animal or two. No other theory could come close to explaining how Ferd got reappointed every four years in spite of his daily demonstration of not having a clue about what he was supposed to be doing. Quite simply, if Ferd wrote a warrant, it was screwed up. Hell, if Ferd put pen to paper, something would be screwed up. Even his name was screwed up. Maybe Ferd forgot where the photos were, who knows, but finally Ferd was canned. He was at least one hundred and fifty years old by then and outraged when he learned the bad news. He could not comprehend how we would get along without his invaluable experience.

I have digressed from Ferd's fugitive warrant. Obviously, the subject of Ferd Hogan still befuddles me. I explained to Ferd on the phone what to write, what warrant to use, and where to find the subject in the code book. He said, "Okay," not "Thank you" — just a grumpy, "Okay," and hung up. Lo and behold, about an hour later, who came in the office but Ferd with the cop and the handcuffed fugitive in tow. Ferd sat down at a typewriter and said in an irritated voice, "Tell me that wording again."

One of the many skills Ferd did not possess was the ability to type. After several abortive tries at typing a comprehensible warrant, Ferd gave it up. He just sat at the typewriter, drumming his fingers, looking vague. Out of sympathy for the cop and the fugitive, who were both looking very worn, I took over. Ferd, looking relieved, got up and scurried out of the office without so much as a "Thank you" or a "Screw you" to me or an apology to the poor cop. Ferd didn't sweat the small stuff.

After my first few days of working with Ferd, I

was desperate to get away from him. During that time, he fell asleep during a citizen's very complicated civil-dispute problem. The citizen was an excitable Asian woman who stormed out of the hearing room, loudly complaining, "He fall asleep. He fall asleep. He no care. He no listen."

He had also said to a woman who was seeking directions about paying a parking ticket, "If you've been raped, you gotta report it to the police." Before I could intervene, the poor woman fled in panic. I never did figure that one out. All my efforts at escape were for naught. Everybody avoided Ferd, and since I was the new kid on the block, I was doomed to spend a prolonged and designated time in the barrel.

Ferd was also incapable of answering the telephone, which seemed to ring ten thousand times a day. I could be listening to testimony, writing a release form, and answering a jailor's question, and if the phone rang, Ferd would continue to laboriously chase a booger around his nose in complete disregard of his surroundings. I did discover that if threatened with physical abuse if he didn't get off his butt and do something, he would condescend to write one or two simple warrants. He would then disappear completely for an hour or two.

During one of these absences, Uncle Billy showed up and asked where Ferd was. I pointed down the hallway to the bathroom and said, "Beats me, Billy. Maybe he's on the bench taking a deposition."

Billy gave me a disapproving look that he seemed to reserve for only me and left, asking no further questions. Even Billy understood that sometimes no Ferd was better than Ferd sitting around with his finger two knuckles deep into his nose.

Chapter 11

Order In the Court

I thought it would be a good idea to follow a few of the cases I had heard through the court system. Nobody had said anything about that end of the matter, but it seemed to me that I should have some idea of what was happening to the cases I was sending to trial. So I picked a few of the more interesting ones I'd done and went to court one day.

The most obvious difference was in the DWI cases. The foul, malodorous, insulting drunks of a few weeks before were now well coiffed, three piece suited, and well coached by tassel-loafered, expensive-looking lawyers. A whole lot of, "Yes, your honor," "No, your honor," "If it would please your honor," was being tossed around like honey-coated horse manure.

As opposed to when I heard these cases, not one DWI claimed to know or be anyone special or important. No one imperiously informed the judge that they would have his job. No one demanded to know the judge's name or the name of his boss. It was hard to imagine these people even knowing any four-letter words, much less, horror of horrors, speaking such vulgarities to a magistrate. My satisfaction, even in cases that did not go the way I thought they should, was in the thousands of dollars some of these people had to fork over to their lawyers to keep their butts out of the slammer. Sometimes they went to the slammer anyway. Very satisfying.

But even in court with its stern bailiffs, robed judges, and intense lawyers, there are hilarious moments. One young man about eighteen-years old was trying to represent himself on a trespassing-on-school-property charge. The judge was attempting to explain to him that if he were found guilty he could be sentenced to jail. He was not having much success. Our young man, I am afraid, had something close to a room-temperature I.Q.

"Do you understand that if I find you guilty of this trespass, you could go to jail?" the judge asked.

"It don't seem that serious, sir."

"You were on the roof of the school during school hours. You scared a lot of people."

"I didn't mean to. I just wanted to visit some of my friends."

"Why not use the door like everyone else?"

The judge had asked what we were all wondering.

A shrug, "I dunno. I guess 'cause they told me last year not to come back."

"Did you graduate?"

"No, sir."

"Can you afford a lawyer?"

"No, sir."

"I guess I'll have to appoint you one," sighed the judge.

"I don't know what that means, sir."

"You frustrate me, son. How far did you get in school, anyway?"

"I was just a few feet in from the edge, sir."

When court begins, the judge explains to the assembled what the process is and what to expect. One admonition usually is, "Do not plead guilty if you don't think you are guilty." After saying that, the judge called the first case, a young man accused of speeding.

"How do you plead?"

"Not guilty."

"What is your defense?"

"I dunno."

"Then why are you pleading not guilty?'

"Because you said to, your honor."

It's hard to argue with logic like that.

Next up was a young man charged with assaulting his girlfriend. He came up to the podium in front of the judge with his arm around a girl. The judged peered over his glasses at the girl and asked, "Are you the complainant?"

She stared at the judge and asked, "What does that mean?"

The judge stared back at her and said, "Did you go to the magistrate and get this warrant?"

"Yes."

I remembered her quite well. She had been one hundred percent positive with me that the relationship was over and she was absolutely going to go to court and testify against what she assured me was now her EX-boyfriend. She did, at least, show up for court.

The judge was not pleased. "Do you want to drop the charge?"

"Yes, your honor, I do."

"Why?"

"We've worked it out."

"What the hell does that mean?" the judge asked, in what I thought was an appropriately menacing tone.

"We're going to get married," the boy volunteered.

"Great," said the judge, "then when you beat on each other you can go to domestic relations court with your *Punch and Judy* show and not waste my time. Dismissed. Get out, and don't come back."

Maybe he wouldn't have to see them again, but I would. No matter what court anybody ends up in, they all start at the magistrate's office.

The next case was nominated by me for the Scumball of the Year award. A somewhat bewildered-looking, nicely dressed, middle-aged woman had been brought to me the day before by the police. They had a warrant from South Carolina requesting she be held by us so they could extradite her for a credit card fraud. I was astounded by her story, which I felt was mostly true.

She, her husband (who was a lawyer), and their three children lived in the area until five years ago. They had moved to a small town in South Carolina, where he had been offered a job with a law firm. As things sometimes go, he began an affair with a woman, who happened to be a judge of the county court. A divorce ensued, the wife was awarded custody of the three children, and he got two weeks visitation in the summer. The now ex-wife and children had moved back to Virginia two years ago.

The affair with the judge continued and the ex-wife settled into what passed for normality in suburbia these days. The day she came before me, the ex-husband had showed up as planned to take the children on a two-week vacation to Colorado. He had arrived at the door, gathered the kids and luggage, put them in the car, and then dropped the bombshell. He introduced her to the two county policemen who had arrived, saying they would be arresting her for a charge in South Carolina.

"Have a nice day." Off he drove.

She explained to me that night, in a quiet, incredulous voice, that the credit card in question was one they obtained and used jointly when they moved. She had destroyed it when she left South Carolina after the divorce. There was no money owed on it at the time.

As I looked at the paperwork the police had given to me, which they had received from South Carolina, I saw she was charged with making false statements to obtain a credit card. That totally confused her, since they had both signed the application together and she was unaware of any false statements made at the time. She had, by now, explained to me about the divorce and the judge and small-town South Carolina folkways.

She said her ex had, of late, been making noises about the amount of the child-support payments. I was baffled. But it all fell into place when I read the judge's name who had issued the warrant. The ex-wife's eyes filled with tears when she heard it and told me it was her ex-husband's lover and the same judge who had caused the marriage to end. I couldn't fathom the exact scheme he was up to, but it stunk worse than one thousand dead South Carolina skunks. I released her for an arraignment in the morning, when she would have to address the extradition matter.

At that hearing, the judge was as disturbed as I had been and told her to take up the matter with South Carolina authorities and to let him know after the matter had been resolved. I'm sorry to say I lost track of the case and don't know the outcome. But it was instructive for me. Is it any wonder people are losing faith in the judicial system and that lawyers are held in such low esteem? These things don't happen only in South Carolina.

The next case was another domestic dispute. The woman had come to me in the middle of the night and her testimony had been spirited, to say the least. "I ain't takin' no mo' f--kin' s--t from him. This ain't right what he done did to me. I want you to lock him up."

What she lacked in eloquence she made up for with graphic description. What he had done did to her was come home that night and demand to know what she had done with the $20 he gave her to buy some food for the baby. Since there was neither food nor the $20 in the house when he got home, he accused her of using it to buy drugs. My assessment of the situation, as I listened to her, was that he was probably right. But everybody lies. In this case, the lie was that he had given her the $20 to buy food. More likely the money was to buy drugs for him, which she did and then snorted it all up herself.

Since that teed him off, he figured he would show her and slugged her two or three times, spit on her, then unzipped his pants and figuratively and literally pissed on her. "Take that, bitch." All this in front of the baby and her five-year-old son. She had definitely been done wrong, and even though half of what she told me was a lie, a warrant was in order.

Two weeks later in court, they strolled down the aisle together as oblivious as if they were in the midway at the county fair. They stood together, swaying, in front of the judge, high as kites. The judge, having seen it too many times before, just shook his head in disgust.

"Are you going to ask me to drop this charge?"

"Yeh, judge."

"If you ever come back into my court under the influence of drugs, I'll find you in contempt. Charge is dropped. Get out of here."

I guess when she told me she wasn't taking any s--t from him, she meant it more literally than I realized. He could piss on her, but he better not s--t on her — maybe.

Over the years I have not spent too much time in court. For the most part, court is deadly boring and it seems to me that the salaries pulled down by general district judges are mostly to coerce them to try to look alert when hearing cases. Some judges find this impossible, though, and feel they have earned their salaries if they manage to stay awake all day. I have a certain amount of sympathy with that. After several hundred DWI's it is pretty hard to show much enthusiasm in listening to testimony such as the following:

"Your honor, I was on routine patrol within the confines of the county when I observed the defendant operating his motor vehicle in what I considered to be an erratic manner. I fell in behind the defendant and observed his vehicle weaving within his lane over a distance of one-half to three-quarters of a mile. During that time, I observed the defendant's left front tire cross over the divided white line five times. At one time, the right side of his automobile crossed completely over the solid yellow line on the right side of the highway. The defendant jerked his automobile back onto the roadway in a very erratic manner. At this time, I made the decision to effect a traffic stop. I proceeded to effect a traffic stop, at which time I approached the automobile and asked to see the defendant's driver's license and registration The defendant seemed somewhat confused, and I observed that his eyes were bloodshot and watery. He had trouble locating his wallet and passed his driver's license several times before handing it to me. I identified the driver as Mr. Smith, the gentleman you see standing before you. I asked Mr. Smith to exit his vehicle, which he did with some difficulty. I administered several field sobriety tests to Mr. Smith. I asked Mr. Smith to count from one hundred to eighty, backward. Mr. Smith did so with difficulty, omitting the numbers ninety-four, ninety-one, eighty-seven, and eighty-three. Mr. Smith also continued to count past the number eighty, not in accordance with my instructions. I next asked Mr. Smith if he had a high school education and if he knew his ABC's. Mr. Smith said he did have a high school education and that he did know his ABC's. I then asked Mr. Smith to recite his ABC's from the letter E through S. Mr. Smith did so in a slow, halting manner, omitting the letters L, P, and R. I then had Mr. Smith perform a finger-dexterity test. I demonstrated the test for Mr. Smith by standing before him with my feet apart and extending my arms horizontally and then bringing one hand toward my face and touching the end of my nose with my index finger. When Mr. Smith attempted to perform the test, under my directions, he consistently touched his upper lip with his finger and quickly moved his finger to the tip of his nose. I then had Mr. Smith perform a leg-balance test. I asked Mr. Smith if he had any leg infirmities to which he replied he did not. I asked Mr. Smith to stand with his arms at his side and to lift whichever leg he wished and to hold that leg in the air in front of him at an approximate forty-five degree angle for a count of twenty. I demonstrated the test for Mr. Smith before allowing him to proceed. Mr. Smith put his leg down at the count of eight. He attempted to repeat the test and put his leg down at the count of six. I then had Mr. Smith perform the walk-and-turn test. I had Mr. Smith stand on the yellow solid line on the side of the road. I instructed Mr. Smith to walk twenty paces away from me placing his heel against his toe while doing so and to leave no spaces between them while staying on the yellow solid line. At the end of twenty paces, Mr. Smith was to turn around and proceed back to me in the same manner. Mr. Smith did not walk heel to toe and there were spaces between his steps. At step numbers four, eight, thirteen and eighteen, Mr. Smith fell off the line completely. Mr. Smith walked back toward me in a normal fashion, not following my instructions to walk heel to toe."

Hour after hour, day after day, week after week, month after month, year after year, listening to such is a Herculean task. Some judges, on occasion, are not up to it. Every defendant expects his case to receive the intense undivided interest of the judge. Mr. Smith, for instance, would understandably be very upset if the judge fell asleep during his trial. It has happened, much to the embarrassment of all parties involved. In one rather infamous case, the judge actually toppled out of his chair and onto the floor. After his honor regained his chair and found the defendant guilty, an appeal was, not surprisingly, duly noted.

Magistrates tend not to fall asleep during such excruciatingly boring testimony, not because of their keen interest, but because they are standing up behind a counter. Even standing, at 300 a.m., there have been times when my interest in the proceedings was such that I had to stop the officer and say I had heard enough to issue a warrant and please not to go on.

Some officers seem to be somewhat offended, others are thankful. Sometimes they bore themselves. If a guy is weaving all over the road, smells like a brewery, and can't stand up, it doesn't make a gnat's ass difference what numbers he misses between eighty and one hundred for me to write a warrant. Let the judge listen to the rest of it. He makes more than I do and doesn't have to work midnights.

It was time to go to Richmond for my training. This was my first experience of working for the government, and I was learning not to be too logical about things. I guess the Army had been government work of a sort and there were certain similarities of thought. But I had expected the Army to be all fouled up, after all, that's where the word snafu originated.

The courts, I was discovering, were also a snafu organization. I had been a magistrate for a few months and had already written more warrants, conducted more bond hearings, and listened to more lies than I could count. Now I was to go to Richmond for a week and learn how I had done it? The explanation given for this bass-ackwards arrangement was that new magistrates would be easier to train if they were familiar with the job. Then, why the training if you already know what you are doing? Maybe Milo Minderbinder would be teaching and explaining some *Catch-22* variations in Richmond. He was not there, and my week of training was a crashing bore. I learned nothing, *nada*, zip, zero. Mike's School of Magistrating had been thorough.

At the end of the week we were asked to submit a critique of the course. I did, complimenting them on their professionalism, but enumerating the problems as I saw them. It was a pretty blunt assessment, and I expected some hostile posturing in return. Their response was, instead, very positive. That certainly never happened in the Army. It seemed a good sign, and I thought that since the job didn't require any heavy lifting, I'd stay with it and see how it went.

Chapter 12

Meeting New Enemies

*B*eing a magistrate, one has to deal directly with the public. The circumstances are usually such that it's not a very *happy* public. If you have been arrested, that's understandable. If you are coming to the magistrate's office seeking help, calling the magistrate odious names is not the recommended approach. I know coming to the jail is not first choice on anybody's list of things to do. I'm not overjoyed about being there myself sometimes — and I'm *paid* to be there. Baring your soul to a complete stranger (me) can be agony. Not getting what you want, such as somebody else arrested, in spite of such soul baring, is a big injury to one's pride and ego. Still, one doesn't have to be a complete jerk about it. Alas, that is more often the case than not. Consider . . .

She seemed a nice enough lady and her fifteen-year-old son seemed no more rebellious than any other teen with his pants halfway down his butt, the crotch at his knees, and his baseball cap on backward. Be that as it may, she said she had talked to the police and she was here so that her son could obtain a warrant for assault. I had them fill out a form and invited them into my office.

"Okay, young man, if you would first of all remove your hat, then I'll put you under oath."

Only mild resentment to that.

"Now, do you swear that everything you're about to tell me is the truth and nothing but the truth?"

"Yeah"

Close enough.

"Now tell me what happened."

"Well, man, me and about ten or twelve of my buddies was minding our own business at the Safeway exit when this old dude came out and — I don't know why, man — but he came over and punched me twice in the face."

Mother had an odd look on her face. A cross between horror and pride?

"Anything else?"

"Naw, man, he just got in his car and drove off."

"What did you do then?"

"We got his tag number, an' I went home, and mom called the cops."

Unbeknownst to mother and son, the police had already called to let me know they had investigated the case and had talked to the "old dude." Apparently, the police had been having trouble with this bunch for quite a while. Their game was to hang out at food stores, drug stores, convenience stores, etc., and generally hassle anybody who didn't look like they would give them any trouble back. They had made a mistake with the "old" dude, who was in his late thirties and, thus, a few years younger than me. I must have seemed older than dirt to this kid.

The old dude had his two teenage daughters with him, which the little twerp now in front of me had failed to mention. Nor did he mention how he had called out to one of them, " Hey, bitch, come sit on my face."

Not surprisingly, that had caused father to want a piece of this kid, and, with some justification, he walked right up to the dirtball and knocked him down with two punches while his buddies scattered. Maybe not the smartest thing to do, but hadn't we all at some time felt the same urge toward a smart-mouthed punk?

I locked eyes with the kid and said, "I want to remind you that you are under oath, and I am asking you if you have told me the whole truth."

"Yeah, why you asking me that?"

"Well, I think what I'm hearing is a sanitized version of events."

Whereupon mother's little boy turned to mama and blurted, "What the f--k does *that* mean?"

Lovely, just lovely. I answered for her. "What it means, you lying little toilet mouth, is no warrant and get out of my office."

Mother was indignant. Not with her perjuring son, but with me. She was outraged. She was going to write her congressman. She was going to write the newspapers. She was going to have justice. Didn't I realize that he would grow up wounded because of this, with no faith in the American system of justice? That if in the future her son ended up in prison because he felt there was no justice, it would be my fault and didn't that bother me?

Since it didn't bother me, I had the deputies escort her out, because she refused to leave unless I had the man arrested. Another dissatisfied customer.

It is, of course, a natural reaction to not like someone who denies you what you want. That's one of the less attractive things about being a magistrate, a lot of people dislike you very much. It should be part of the job description: "Work weird hours, receive generous abuse, meet new enemies."

Deny someone a warrant, he hates you passionately. Issue someone a warrant, then the accused hates you with equal fervor. Tell some young girl, for instance, that you can't prohibit her ex-boyfriend from coming within five million miles of her for the rest of his life, and she'll tell you that you're a sexist pig and taking the man's side. And a twerp, too.

Most decisions that you make mean at least one side will be demanding your head on a platter. Sometimes both sides demand it. Letters are written, complaints are lodged, satisfaction demanded. As I once said to the chief magistrate, "If you never get involved, no one will ever complain about you. It's a little like a basketball game. If you don't have four fouls on you by the fourth quarter, then you haven't been doing anything."

Chapter 13

Bon Apetit

I mentioned earlier of the relative ease in dealing with the hard-core criminal as opposed to the drunk. That doesn't mean that they're nice people. Many of them are dangerous, vicious thugs with absolutely no concern for anyone but themselves. They have no morals or shame, commit frightful crimes, and if caught, consider jail time just a hazard of doing business. Dealing with the habitual criminal is usually a straightforward, low-key, nonemotional affair.

At the magistrate level — the first encounter with a judicial officer — it is understood by the crook that it's dumb to bad-mouth the magistrate. Long hours on rotating shifts do not make magistrates overly friendly. Bad timing, such as getting arrested at the beginning of a long weekend, combined with a bad attitude, and it might be days under a substantial bond before seeing a judge. Of course, some bad guys realize they're not going anywhere — no matter what.

Yet in twelve years of dealing with murderers, robbers, burglars, and thieves, rarely has one of them
been abusive or given me a hard time.

The drunk has called me every foul name imaginable and unimaginable, some of which I wasn't sure
of the meaning. We had a new woman magistrate of
gentle birth, who after a week said to me in wonderment, "This week I've been called what I believe to be
medical terms I was unaware existed."

Another magistrate, after his first midnight shift
of dealing with drunks, was heard to comment, "I lost
count of the number of times last night I was told to
perform what I'd call an anatomically impossible sex
act." It was postulated to him that it was a sign of the
decline of educational standards that nothing much
more imaginative than, "Go f--k yourself," was being
heard so often. Of course, we do get the occasional
teacher in, but they are a generally well-behaved lot,
so I rarely broach the subject with them. They at least
have the decency to be embarrassed about their situation; both their present one before me and the general
one at the school house.

Not so the habitual crook. Arraignments, trials,
jail time, parole, and probation are just a part of his
life. No big deal. Just do what the man says and get
back to business when you get out. No resentment,
no remorse. Business as usual. Go to jail. Get another tattoo. Lift some weights. No time clock, no
boss, hot-and-cold running water. Three hots and a
cot. Conditions inside for many of them are better
than those outside. Some are not so sure which side
they'd rather have, but none will ever admit it.

A young woman was brought before me one day

by a jailor about a week before Thanksgiving. She would finish her sentence in the jail that night for bad check charges. However, the jailor had two teletypes: one from Prince Georges County, Maryland, and one from Montgomery County, Maryland. Both counties wanted to extradite her for credit card offenses. I could write a fugitive-from-justice warrant for one but not both. Before I could decide which county to send her to, the woman asked to speak.

"Sir, if I waive extradition in the morning before the arraignment judge, how long will it be before Maryland comes and gets me?"

"Two days."

"Could you please write the warrant for Prince Georges County then?"

"I can if you want. It makes no difference to me. But why?"

" I know I'll be in jail over Thanksgiving, and since the Prince Georges County jail food is much better than Montgomery County, I'd like to be there instead." She gave me a sweet smile from ear to ear. Her arrest record was several pages long, and she probably understood the extradition process better than I did. She certainly knew jail cuisine better. She was quite pleasant, almost endearing, and was in jail because she would steal anything that wasn't bolted down. I granted her request, wrote the warrant, and wished her "*Bon apetit!*"

Another holiday story about incorrigibles involves a Texan. About five years before I met up with Tex, he was convicted in Dallas of a burglary. He served a year or two and was paroled, whereupon he immediately broke his parole and came to Virginia looking for work. Things were tough in Texas at the time, and his parole officer probably would have approved his move if Tex had asked. But being from Texas, he just didn't feel he needed to ask. He got a job and all was well until Christmas season arrived and Tex began to miss his mother and daddy in Dallas. He didn't have enough money to take the bus home, but he did have a brainstorm. He turned himself in to the police and told them he was a parole violator.

Sure enough, Texas sent a teletype saying they would extradite, and, sure enough, Tex was back in Dallas for Christmas where his parents could visit him in jail. All paid for by the great state of Texas. About a month later he was released by the judge and admonished to keep in better contact with his parole officer. There was still no work in Texas so, of course, Tex came back to Virginia and, of course, he didn't tell his parole officer. Christmas came again. Tex started feeling blue again.

It's happened three years in a row now, and whenever the Texas authorities arrive, Tex goes out of our jail chained hand and foot, all smiles, one happy cowboy going home for the holidays.

Chapter 14

"Y" for Asian

The magistrate's office is certainly a place of irreverence and gallows humor. It could be nothing else. One needs a shield, a defense, a way to cope with the broken lives and bodies, lost hope, alcoholism, drug addiction, rape, murder, mental illness, child molestation, suicide. If magistrates became personally involved in all these tragedies, they'd be destroyed. As it is, we become too personally involved in too many lives just to get the job done. The intimate details of peoples lives I have to know in order to write warrants and set bonds are an occupational hazard. I have to ferret out information from people that they wouldn't tell their wives, husbands, or mothers. Some of the depths I plumb can produce unnerving answers.

I refuse to become a cynic, which means I still have to care; and I do. I am selective and allow myself to become involved only when there is hope that

I can do some good. Balanced against the desire to do good is the knowledge that you can't save all the puppies in the world. It seems to be the general feeling of all the magistrates. Those who don't work out this balancing act don't last. Burnout is common, and a high number of magistrates resign in either disgust or despair. Do the best you can, but don't go down with the ship.

Maintaining a detached demeanor in every case is just not possible or desirable. When the mother of two toddlers came to see the magistrate about her fast-food, drive-through window episode, she told a story that my colleague absorbed in wonderment. She related how she had placed a breakfast order for her two young children and drove to the pickup window. There, she realized she had ordered orange juice when she meant apple juice, and she asked the woman to change it. It seemed a simple enough request. The clerk had a drastically different opinion about it.

She glared at mom in outraged disapproval and replied in a distinctly un-customer-friendly tone, "F--k you!"

Mom, still in shock, decided she could not possibly have heard correctly and just laid the bills and coins on the counter. Must have said, "Thank you," or maybe, "Up to you."

Alas, no. For as she was thinking that, the woman, who was in her mid-thirties, hurled the coins and another very distinct "F--k you" at mom and disappeared. Completely bewildered as to what to do next, the mother was horrified to see the clerk rush out a side door screaming as she began furiously kicking the front of her car. Almost immediately, a man came charging out the same door and without hesitation tackled the girl! As mom watched, still in shock, they wrestled and slugged it out, rolling around on the driveway. Her children, understandably scared by it all, were screaming and crying. An added problem — the man wasn't very big, and he wasn't winning the fight.

To mom's dismay, the man, who was now in a headlock in the bushes, pulled out a cell phone and tossed it through her car window, yelling in a strangled voice, "I'm the manager! Call the police! Call the police!"

She didn't know how to use the phone, and the fight continued. Soon, both of them were partway under the car, which brought a lull in the fray. The manager, lying on the ground, saw that mom was staring down at them in horror and began apologizing profusely, even though the girl's hands were wrapped around his neck.

"So sorry, so sorry. She has problems. She gets angry sometimes. She has problems."

One problem she didn't have was not knowing how to fight. She was doing a job on the manager. Fortunately, before he was seriously injured, the police arrived. Someone in the restaurant did know how to use a cell phone.

Problems or not, sorry or not, it didn't matter to mom. She wanted something done about the hellcat. She'd been hit in the face by the change, her children had been terrified, and her car was dented. A vice-president of the company had already tried to contact her to say the clerk was fired and to please call him back. Mom might have been right when she said, "Probably wants to promise me a lifetime supply of French fries or something."

The clerk did get charged with assault and damage of property. Whatever her problems were, it was for the judge to sort out at trial.

After the warrants were issued, my partner said to her it was certainly one of the oddest cases he had ever heard, and that it was especially surprising because of the high premium put on customer relations by the fast-food industry. She nodded slowly in agreement while wearily putting on her coat, "Yes, I suppose you're right," she sighed. "What a day. Whoever would have thought all this over breakfast for two kids. Well, at least I did learn something. Next time I'll just take the damned orange juice."

As often occurs, more than one case is being heard at the same time in the office. I was not able to hear the fast-food caper, because I was handling a case that was both irritating and amusing. A trooper who I knew to be a Vietnam veteran had come in with a Vietnamese under arrest for a driving offense of some type.

"Sir, I don't know if this guy is trying to be smart with me or what, but it says right here on his license that his name is Nguyen. Now I've been to Vietnam, and I know a little bit about their language, and I know this name is pronounced Nu-gen. He keeps grinning at me and saying it's like the word 'win'. I think he's trying to hide something."

I thought it best not to suggest that the trooper's pronunciation was certainly the 1st Cavalry Americanized version. I did say that Mr. Nguyen probably knew how to pronounce his own name. The trooper didn't look convinced. The only other "win" he knew was baseball pitcher Early Wynn, and he sure as hell wasn't Vietnamese. The trooper seemed to think there was great significance to the matter. I finally had to tell him that he wasn't the pronunciation police, and we moved on to testimony about the traffic charge. The first Vietnamese named Phuc or Dong that the trooper might encounter would in all probability also have some touch questioning about their pronunciations.

Race is a topic during testimony because any resulting arrest warrants, among other things, designate the race of the accused. Thus, the discussion of someone's race isn't the taboo it is in so many other environments, where even the mention of the words white, black, Asian, or Hispanic makes people uncomfortable.

A new Vietnamese officer was all smiles one day, even though he had a pretty unruly drunk under arrest. When I asked why the smile, he beamed, "I feel like a real cop now. He keeps saying the only reason I arrested him is because he's Hispanic and I'm a racist. I've never been called a racist before."

I said, "Yeh, kinda brings a tear to your eye, doesn't it? Sort of a rite of passage."

Citizens seeking a warrant have to fill out a form on the accused asking for name, date of birth, sex, race, address, etc. Sometimes people leave race blank. Usually, it is because the accused is either East Indian, or Middle-eastern, or Hispanic, and the person isn't sure what to write.

I explain to them that it is not really a racial designation, but more a description to give the police who will be serving the warrant an idea of what the person looks like. East Indians can confuse people because some are very dark skinned but have distinct Caucasoid features. They usually end up "W" for white, since the computer accepts only W, B and O for white, black, and oriental. One day, though, a Korean came in and in the block put the letter Y.

I looked at him and asked, "Why Y?"

He spread his hands and with a wonderful smile said, "Black, white, yellow."

He wanted a warrant for an Asian, and it was hard to fault his logic.

On another occasion an older lady had put "C" in the block. In the old, old days "C" stood for colored, and once in a while someone, usually older, will still use it. I can never be sure so I asked if the "C" was for Caucasian. She laughed and said yes, and that she had worked for the Marine Corps for many years filing incident reports that required race and Caucasian was what was used. She was always forgetting that "W" was preferred now. She apologized for laughing but said it reminded her of a phone call she had received many years ago when the mother of a Marine had called and was irate about the incident report involving her son. It was gently explained to her that it was only a minor traffic accident on base and was really not a very big deal and nothing to be so upset about.

The mother, who by her accent, was from deep in the Appalachian Mountains, was not interested in that. She had another bone to pick. "In this report here, you've got my boy's race listed as Caucasian. And you ain't got that right. I'm a callin' to tell you my boy ain't no Caucasian, he's white."

Chapter 15

Bang, You're Dead

Death hits you right in the face. No matter how it arrives, accidental or intentional, it commands the scene. In the middle of the night, a state trooper stops a weaving automobile on the interstate. When the driver gets out of the car, he is obviously intoxicated. Nothing unusual until the trooper notices a pair of legs showing under a pile of newspapers and beer cans in the front seat. He asks who it is, and the man says it's his wife. When the trooper tells the man to wake her up, he says she won't wake up, ever — she's dead. Only then does the trooper notice the blood and brains all over the inside of the passenger door.

Before my first cup of coffee on Monday morning, the trooper presented me with this. He was exhausted, having worked the case most of the night. I was barely awake, trying to comprehend the enormity of what I was hearing. Apparently, the man and his wife were separated, but on Sunday morning she agreed to go for a ride with him to talk about it. He picked her up outside New York City, drove to a secluded spot and shot her repeatedly in the head. Then for the next eighteen or so hours, he drove aimlessly around New York, New Jersey, Pennsylvania, Maryland, and Virginia, drinking beer and reading the Sunday *New York Times*. Empty beer cans and discarded newspaper sections were flung contemptuously on top of her body.

By the time the man was brought to me, he was sobering up. It had been about four hours since being stopped by the trooper. He was an average-looking guy in his mid-fifties. He was somewhat agitated but completely cooperative as I explained that I'd be charging him with murder and holding him for New York authorities to interview. He had never been in trouble before. Worked at the same company his entire adult life while raising a family. Brought his paycheck home each week and paid his mortgage each month. The separation from his wife had apparently ripped loose his moral anchor. How close to the breaking point many unknowingly are.

Domestic-violence cases are always hard to understand and extremely difficult to handle. It is frightening how a person who at one time loved somebody, slept in the same bed, and raised children together, could come to detest them so much as to commit murder. The venom and bitterness in these people is sometimes obvious. In others it is hidden, even from themselves.

The police once brought a doctor before me who had just stabbed his wife to death in their kitchen.

He was very distraught and told me he had tried to stay away from her all day because he knew if they talked any, something would happen. Their problems did not seem that overwhelming. They had grown distant from each other after their children moved out. There had never been any violence before. He seemed a very mild-mannered guy. Then something in him snapped and, suddenly, she was dead. He stood in front of me, shaking his head in disbelief. He couldn't believe that he had done such a monstrous thing. He was as surprised as anybody.

Others plan carefully. A woman called her husband, who was living in Utah, and asked him to fly out so they could talk about the final divorce decree coming up. She told him to call when he got to the airport so she would know when to expect him. He agreed, hoping this would be the last time they would have to meet. When he showed up at the door, she shot him six times with a gun she had bought specifically for the occasion. When she bought the gun, she had even asked the salesman to point out the area of the body that was best for a killing shot. After she pumped the six rounds into him, she closed and locked the door and went to bed. Police, summoned by neighbors about the sound of gunshots, found him dead on the front step. Even in prison she claimed to have slept through the whole thing and knew nothing about it.

On another occasion, a man came to the public lobby at the magistrate's office and told me he had just had a domestic dispute with his wife and he thought the police might want to talk to him. I told him to have a seat and I'd check. The police, I discovered, wanted to talk to him very much in light of the fact that he had just caught her in the parking lot of her office on the way to work and in front of twenty witnesses, stabbed her through the heart. He had then driven off to his favorite bar and had a few drinks while calmly describing the event to the bartender, who had a friend who was a magistrate. The bartender convinced him to come on down and see us.

He and his wife had been separated for several years, although he visited occasionally. When he stopped by the night before, she wasn't home. He sat on the front step all night drinking beer and brooding, but she never came home. When morning arrived, he decided to catch her at work. According to the witnesses, when she got out of her car she saw him walking toward her and started running immediately. He ran her down and did the deed without hesitation, never saying a word to her.

I have never dwelled too much on the different reactions I have to these deaths. Perhaps I should, since a few, amazingly, seem to have a small bit of humor in them. Death and humor are not words often used together. Before becoming a magistrate, I never used them together.

One day, a traffic accident investigator walked in and said to me, "Do you know anything about marine biology?"

"Can't say I do."

"The medical examiner is all pissed off at me for asking him the same question."

Alerted by an odd smile on his face, I asked suspiciously, "Are you going to tell me something I don't really want to hear?"

"Maybe, maybe not."

"Go away."

"Hey, I had a D.O.A. in a traffic accident, and she was five feet three inches tall, five hundred and forty-five pounds. I just thought at the autopsy, some marine biology experience would be helpful."

I guess if you investigate traffic deaths every day, you get weird.

One night on Route 1, a drug deal went wrong and one bad guy killed another. After investigating the case and identifying the trigger man from witnesses, the detective came to me and asked, "Can I get a misdemeanor murder warrant for this guy."

I thought it a poor joke and told him so.

Doing a bad job of looking contrite, the detective said, "Sorry, sir, not a good suggestion. The possibility of jail time does seem a little severe. Maybe I could just make do with this parking ticket here. Yeah, here we go — time expired — ten dollars." Cynicism has always been epidemic in police work.

Humor and death, though, are just not comfortable companions. There was only tragedy and horror in the case I handled of a mother killing her two young daughters. She calmly set them and her house on fire, then called the police to tell them what she had done. At the arraignment she was unfocused, confused, bewildered. I had the feeling she had lost her way long before and that this was the end of a tortured journey. Why had no one noticed? Then, who can possibly understand the terrifying torment and writhing nightmares going on in the depths of such a person's mind.

She was sent for a psychiatric evaluation, eventually adjudged insane and incapable of standing trial.

The outrageous case of a young baby-sitter who, losing her temper, killed a one-year-old by throwing it ten feet across the room into a crib was maddening. She showed no remorse that I could discern. It just didn't seem to affect her. When I talked to her a few hours after the killing, I thought her nonchalant attitude was a residual symptom of shock and her defiance a shield to hide feelings of guilt. It was not so. She just didn't think it was her fault. It was as if the child were responsible for its own death. Too bad the kid was dead, but she just didn't feel responsible.

My saddest moment ever involved a young Hispanic man who had been arrested for being drunk. The police had responded to a call about some unknown activity in a cemetery in the middle of the night. They found this young man, distraught, in tears, beside himself with grief, trying to drink away the sadness beside his three-year-old daughter's recent grave. The police were afraid to leave him there alone, so they brought him to me. Through the tears, which he was unable to stop, he kept quietly apologizing for inconveniencing us. His wife was at home, equally heartbroken and alone. They needed to be with each other, and I had him taken there. It saddens me to this day when I think about him.

Chapter 16

It Always Gets Worse

*P*erhaps even more incomprehensible than murder and death, if that's possible, is to utilize one's own children, to even abuse and discard them, if need be, to even get back at a spouse in divorce proceedings.

A woman came to see me one Friday night with her three children, of whom she was very solicitous. They were aged seven, nine, and eleven. She didn't know what else to do, she told me tearfully. She had just discovered from her children that all three had been sexually molested over the years by their father, whom she was divorcing. I had been a magistrate several years by this time and had dealt with many such divorce/molestation cases, sad to say. I immediately smelled a rat.

The children all dutifully told me that, indeed, it was true: their father had been doing awful things to them. I didn't want these children to give me any details. They had already been through enough, if my suspicions were true. I stopped the hearing, excused myself from the room, immediately checked the circuit-court records, and talked to someone at child-protective services. Bingo! That very afternoon, the circuit court had awarded complete custody of the children to the father after a very long, bitter custody battle. Her many previous allegations of abuse had been found by protective services to be completely false. She was to turn the children over to the father the next day.

Whether she had threatened the children or promised them rewards of candy and presents to tell the lie, I didn't know. I had seen it done both ways. I returned to the hearing room, sat down, stared at her hard, and said, "I believe the custody ordered by the circuit court this afternoon will stand."

All pretense of concern for her darling children immediately disappeared. She roughly herded them outside in the cold and dark and then returned to rage at me. It was one of the quickest Jekyll-and-Hyde transformations I had ever seen. If her children were cornered outside by knife-wielding molesters, I don't think she would have lifted a finger in their defense. Once their usefulness as victims — to get their father locked up — evaporated, so did her concern for them. They were extremely nice kids who didn't have a clue about what was really going on.

I firmly escorted her out of the office. I was incensed that she had left the children alone in the cold and dark like that, and I was not going to listen to any insults from that contemptible woman. As I watched out the window, she stormed across the parking lot with her three little children running behind her, barely able to keep up. It was a heartbreaking scene.

An officer came to me one evening with a case that rated high on the slimeball scale of domestic dirty tricks. An American woman had married an Iranian, and the marriage had produced two children. The marriage had, after a few years, dissolved due to the husband's habit of beating his wife. Custody of the children had been awarded to her.

The next year, after a medical examination, there was a suspicion that the mother might have breast cancer. A biopsy was being done on the day the officer saw me. While the mother was at the hospital, the father, who had paid child support on a sporadic basis, showed up at the house and kidnapped the children, who were six and seven. He told the mother's sister, who struggled with the man, that they were going to Iran and nobody would see the children again. She called the police, but he was gone when they arrived. How despicable can one be?

The cop had worked his butt off by the time he came to me. Not only had he ascertained that there was a flight out of J.F.K. in New York to Teheran with the father and children booked on it that evening, but he had also traced them to an Amtrak train, which was at that moment on the way to New York. He also made Amtrak police aware of the situation. The officer asked me to issue a kidnapping warrant based on the custody order, which he had also managed to obtain and verify. In addition, he had also received authorization from a commonwealth's attorney for extradition if I issued a warrant. It was a very impressive performance of efficiency and initiative.

I issued the warrant, everything fell into place, and the Amtrak police arrested the flabbergasted father when the train pulled into Philadelphia. The children were returned home within a few hours. It was a satisfying conclusion to a nasty piece of business. Sad to say that such conclusions are extremely rare, which made this one particularly sweet.

The vast majority of domestic violence cases are committed by men on women. It is still amazing to me the amount of abuse and beatings women will take before doing anything about it. For some women, it's one punch and that's it. It's all over for the guy. Sad to say the majority take it for years. It is not my job as a magistrate to be an advocate for battered women, but many have been the times that I have wanted to encourage a woman to get an assault warrant when she seemed to be wavering. I know all too well that if the beating is allowed to continue, it always gets worse.

Today, due to a police department policy change, if an officer feels an assault has occurred, he can make an arrest without the victim concurring. Before that policy was instituted, if the victim wouldn't sign a warrant, the police could do nothing. I understand the reluctance of some women. Fear of being alone, no money, no place to go, no food for the children, fear of retaliation. When does one say enough is enough? Yet some cases are so extreme they defy understanding.

The police brought to me a nineteen-year-old woman, eight months pregnant. She was bleeding from the head, had an eye swollen shut, and teeth knocked out. She looked like she had been in a car

wreck. In fact, her boy friend had beaten her senseless and had even kicked her repeatedly in the side
with his work boots on as she lay on the floor. Her
lips were so cut and swollen it was hard for her to
speak.

The police were holding the boyfriend in the
magistrate's lobby in anticipation of an arrest warrant being issued. This was before the change in police policy. A female officer sat with her in my office.
It was one of the worst beatings I'd seen in a long
while. Most barroom brawls don't turn out this bad.
To my complete astonishment, she wouldn't sign a
warrant. The female officer pleaded and even begged.
Failing that, she then tried shaming her into sign-
ing the warrant.

"You're eight months pregnant. If not for you, do it
to protect your child."

"I can't do it," she mumbled through swollen lips
and broken teeth.

"If you won't do it, we'll have to let him go, and he'll
just beat you some more," the cop truthfully told her.

"He's good to me most of the time."

The cop and I exchanged amazed glances.

"Ma'am," I said, "you've been sitting here for half
an hour refusing to sign a warrant. You should really
be in a hospital. We can't sit here all day. You need to
sign this warrant."

She blew me completely out of the water when
she replied in a strong voice of finality, "I ain't gonna
sign no warrant. What I really want you to do is tell
him to stop f--kin' my mama. If'n he'd stop doing
that, things would be all right."

I thought the cop's eyes were going to bug out of

her head. I'm sure I looked stunned. I finally managed to recover enough to say something about that
not being what we were all here about.

She stood up, rather shakily, and said, "If you
won't talk to him about that, then I'm leaving."

Incredibly, she and her boyfriend left together,
arms around each other, she still bleeding. Only an
hour before he had almost killed her. The officer stood
in the doorway with hot tears of anger and frustration on her cheeks, watching them walk away across
the parking lot. She was rigid and tensed, fists and
teeth clenched. "Eight months pregnant and the ignorant bitch doesn't give a damn that he almost killed
her and the baby. He's doing her mother, and she's
mad because mama likes it and he won't stop. God,
what a world."

Chapter 17

Little Darlings

I had a twenty-one-year-old Ford F-250 stake-body truck I kept in my barn. It had less than 30,000 miles and was in beautiful condition. Yesterday I discovered it had been vandalized by some kids who broke into the barn and with a BB gun shot out the windshield, headlights, side mirrors, and passenger-side door window. They poured roofing tar on the hood and paint thinner down an air vent and broke several running lights. I suppose I should consider myself lucky they didn't burn down my one hundred-year-old barn. They probably would have if they had thought of it. My neighborhood is mostly five-acre lots with at least $500,000 homes. Mine's not one of those, by the way.

We're not talking about disadvantaged, deprived children here. Punks is the word that comes most readily to mind. Even if it were possible to tell who the punks were, their parents would in all probability deny even the possibility that their little darlings could do such things. I see that reaction time and again at court. Consider these juvenile (read "punk") cases:

Two sets of parents arrived at my office one night, demanding that I issue arrest warrants for several people at a drunken party who had cruelly assaulted and kidnapped their fourteen-year-old sons. Of course, as usual, it was going to be my ass if I didn't do this immediately because they were very important people — as usual. According to the parents, their boys were doing a nature study in a rowboat on a pond that is surrounded by homes, when suddenly, out of nowhere, they were attacked and dragged to shore and held by some drunken animals until the police arrived and freed the tykes.

The two children were traumatized and very distraught over such a ghastly incident. Are the children of America not safe anywhere? I told the very important people that they would have to wait in the lobby while I contacted the officer who was first on the scene and who had called the very important parents down to pick up their sons. Officer Drew, who in the past had always impressed me with her professionalism, called me right back.

"I was expecting your call," she said. "I'm sorry you're having to talk to those people, but I can't tell them they can't see you."

"That's quite all right. That's what I'm here for. So tell me the real story, which I presume is somewhat at odds with their version, since you're not here helping them obtain these warrants for felonies, high crimes, and misdemeanors."

The real story is that several retired people in their

sixties and seventies were having a cookout in a neighbor's backyard that borders on the pond. About ten at night, from out of the dark, rocks, mud, and unidentified debris began raining down on these people from the direction of the pond. One elderly woman was struck in the leg and cut. One of the guests was able to barely see something off in the dark on the water. He and some other guests followed what turned out to be a boat, and when it eventually came to shore, they grabbed the two teens and held them down until the police arrived.

The police, after interviewing everyone, called the boys' parents to come and get them and advised the parents that their kiddies were being charged with assault. The boat had also been "borrowed," but the boat owner didn't want to pursue charges, probably out of fear of being sued by the parents, times being what they are today. Of course, the very important parents were outraged. Not with their kids, oh no, but with the police for allowing their babies to be roughed up by the dastardly senior citizens. As Officer Drew said to me, "If someone threw rocks at my grandmother and hurt her, I'd have done a whole lot worse to those two little s--ts than just hold them down in the mud."

I concurred in spades and returned to the very important parents.

"Don't you think ten at night is a little late for a nature study?"

They exchanged furtive glances.

One mother, either braver or dumber than the others, sallied forth with, "My child was stalked and attacked. I want these people punished."

"Officer Drew has interviewed everyone there and

feels the boys should be charged with assault. I will rely on Officer Drew's investigation and will not issue any warrants to you. You were not there and are relying solely on what your son's side of the story is. I would have to consider his view somewhat biased."

It was like kicking a hornet's nest.

"How dare you call my son a liar! It's the officer who is biased. She's the one who's lying. This is an outrage. You've not heard the end of this . . ."

You get the idea. Lovely people. The two budding naturalists were eventually convicted of assault. But I'm sure it had no beneficial effect on them as, no doubt, the parents assured them repeatedly that it was a miscarriage of justice and probably bought them new stereo systems to soothe and protect their injured egos. One assault conviction doesn't stand a chance against years of neglect, no discipline, and no guidance.

Perhaps the most amazing juvenile case I ever encountered involved a seven-year-old girl. One evening, Officer Marvin called with the ominous question of how old must a child be to be charged with a criminal act. I knew immediately that I shouldn't have answered the phone and briefly considered putting the officer on hold and telling my partner that the call was for him. Since he's six feet and four inches tall and weighs two hundred and twenty pounds and I'm not, I asked Officer Marvin cautiously, "Why do you ask?"

"Well, I know she's only seven, but I think the brat needs to be charged with something. And the homeowners involved in this thing are calling me asking what I'm going to do. And the seven-year-old's parents' lawyer is calling me, too."

I was beginning to think I might risk six feet and four inches, two hundred and twenty pounds. "And why are you calling me?"

Definite stress in Officer Marvin's voice, "Because no one else knows what to do, and I've got to do something."

I was doing a mental duck and weave, since handling seven-year-old criminals sounded a bit dicey. Believing in the adage that it's hard to hit a moving target, I tried my verbal Ali shuffle, "Shouldn't you be talking to your supervisor about how to handle this?"

"I have, and he said to ask you what to do."

It looked like I was in imminent danger of suffering a TKO. Time to quit shuffling and act like a judicial officer. "Tell me the story."

The neighbors of the seven-year-old had been transferred and had put their house up for sale. They had to move before the house was sold. For some reason, the seven-year-old didn't like the neighbors and broke into the house through a rear glass door, looking for mischief and taking along an eight-year-old playmate. What she found were several paint cans, which she opened, and she threw paint all over the walls, carpet, and appliances.

Then she found some rags in a can, which she put a match to. It never became clear what she intended to do with that. But the fire scared her, so she threw the can in the kitchen sink, turned on the water, and ran out the back door. The water did put the fire out but the burned rags stopped the drain and the water ran for three days until the real estate agent came in on a routine check. The net result was over $50,000 of damage to the hardwood floors, walls, and electrical wiring. The eight-year-old friend, who had watched but not participated, after a week of feeling guilty told her mother what had happened. Mother, doing the right thing, notified the police, and Officer Marvin was the unfortunate one assigned to handle the report.

Old English common law does, in fact, consider seven-year-olds prosecutable for criminal acts. Officer Marvin wasn't sure that was what she wanted to hear. What I suggested to the officer was to go to the commonwealth's attorney's office and present the case to them. After all, if it was going to be pursued, their office would have to prosecute it. If they agreed to prosecute, go for it. If they chose not to, tell all interested parties to take it up with the commonwealth's attorney's office themselves.

I suppose I weaseled out of the decision somewhat, but I wasn't about to charge a seven-year-old girl in pigtails with a felony unless someone was going to prosecute the case. As it turned out, they did agree to prosecute but screwed it up. In court, the girl's parents agreed to pay for damages to the house if the case was dropped. It appeared there would be a satisfactory resolution, but due to a procedural error, the case was dismissed before the parents legally agreed to pay damages. Their lawyer, seeing the opening, advised them not to pay. They were only too happy to take his advice. The case ended up in civil court with an out-of-court settlement. Their refusal to abide by their initial court agreement showed a lack of moral character, which apparently they were passing on to their daughter at an early age. I never did hear what the daughter had against the neighbors.

Chapter 18

Lost In Translation

I was puzzling over a particularly arcane piece of legislation when an Asian woman came to the window and stared at me. Nonplussed over the intent of the legislature, I was happy enough to give it up, and went over to her and said, "What can I do for you?"

She looked me dead in the eye and said, "You suck."

I've had worse things said to me, but there is usually at least some small hint that it's coming. To the best of my recollection, I had not insulted or disparaged this woman ever before. I didn't think I had even seen her before.

Thinking perhaps she was a nut case, I humored her. "Have we been introduced?"

To which she smiled in an odd sort of way and said, "Suck you."

So where do we stand now, I thought. "Look," I

said, "we went over and fought a war for you all and saved your asses. Is this the thanks we get?" Or maybe it was a war *against* them. I wasn't sure since she could have been Chinese, Japanese, Korean, or Vietnamese.

To which she smiled and said, "I look for suck you."

This was getting pretty damned weird. I looked at my partner for help. He looked at her, shrugged, and said, "She's not my type," and went back to reading his G. Gordon Lidy newsletter.

About that time a deputy came by and handed me a list of people scheduled to be released from jail at midnight, which was only a few minutes away. As I absentmindedly looked it over, trying to figure out what the hell was wrong with this woman, a name jumped out at me: Suk, Yoo. I held the list up and pointed the name out to her.

She beamed a huge smile and nodding vigorously said, "Yes, Suk Yoo, my husband, yes, yes."

Frequently, the King's English takes quite a beating from supposedly native speakers. In Maryland, there is a judicial officer similar to a magistrate called a commissioner. So, some people from Maryland show up at our office asking to see the magistrator. I always smile, as it makes me think of a clothes washer. "Can I see an automatic, front-loading magistrator?"

I have heard about the age of "aquariums" from a young hippie under the influence of something, the sex act as "forniculating," and an illegitimate son a "bastion." A person ordered to pay restitution thought the judge meant "prostitution" and ended up at our office asking how to get started. That was a very strange conversation.

"The judge ordered me to pay by prostitution."

"Excuse me?"

"What do I do now? Everything went so fast in court, I don't know what I'm supposed to do."

"I wasn't in court, ma'am, but I kinda doubt that's what he ordered."

"The judge said he was making 'prostitution' part of the sentence."

It was a struggle, but I finally convinced her that all she had to do was pay the complainant for the windshield that she broke — restitution.

She said, "Oh," and wandered out. Maybe I'd disappointed her, who knows.

I was listening to testimony one day from a state trooper who had been transferred from the southwestern part of the state. He had arrested a trucker for driving on a suspended license and hauling a load of dry ice that had fallen on the road. Or so I thought. When he had finished his testimony I asked, "Did the dry ice cause any accidents?"

Both the trooper and the trucker looked at me as if I had just dropped in from Mars. It seemed like a perfectly legitimate question to me, and I didn't see any reason for confusion. I asked again, "Dry ice. He was hauling dry ice, right?"

The trooper was really concentrating, trying to follow me. "Uh, no, sir." He and the trucker exchanged glances.

I was getting frustrated. "Isn't that why you stopped him? His load of dry ice fell on the road?"

The trooper was at a loss. "No, sir. I pulled him over because his marker lights were out."

The trucker spoke a dialect of English somewhat closer to mine than that of the trooper. That, apparently, allowed him to work out the problem first. "Sir, if I may say something?"

"By all means, please do."

"What I'm hauling, sir, is a load of dry asphalt." The trucker was choosing his words very carefully here. He didn't want to get on the wrong side of anybody. "I believe maybe, sir, you thought you heard the trooper here say he saw my load of 'dry ice' fall, but I think what he said was he saw my load was dry *asphalt*."

I knew now how our Vietnamese magistrate felt. He had learned his English while picking apples in Pennsylvania and had eventually gone on to earn a masters degree in psychology. His second job had been in Richmond, Virginia. When he arrived, to his dismay, he was barely able to understand a word that was said and practically had to learn the language all over. I didn't think the trooper ever did see the problem that day. Ice fall, asphalt, it all sounded the same, and he got his warrant. That's all he wanted anyway.

One of my more complete communications breakdowns occurred when a deaf, mute woman came to the window one day. She was communicating in sign language with her two teenage sons. I communicated with her by the laborious writing of questions and answers on a note pad while her two sons looked on. Her third son had been arrested and was in jail for a minor traffic charge. I discovered, after a very long time of passing notes back and forth, that she owned her home, had a good job, had lived in the area for many years, and that the son was a pretty good kid who had never previously been in trouble. I decided to release him to her. My handwriting is atrocious. Sometimes I can't read it myself, so I had to write very carefully and slowly in order for her to be able to read it. After half an hour of it, I felt exhausted. If it frustrated me having to communicate this way, she had to do it every day.

The deputies brought the boy over and, as I was explaining to him the papers he had to sign, a thought entered my head which surprisingly did not die of loneliness in my empty noggin. He wasn't hearing impaired at all and answered everything in a clear, concise voice. I went out to the lobby and walked up to one of the other two sons and said, "Do you understand that I'm saying?"

"Sure do," he answered clearly

"During that whole time your mother and I were writing notes you never said a word. Why not?"

"Nobody asked me anything, sir."

It sort of left me speechless.

I spent about fifteen minutes one day trying to find a name in the computer for an African woman who spoke heavily accented English — and spoke it poorly. The last name sounded like Artis with the accent on the second syllable, but there was no one in jail by that name. I had her pronounce it again. Maybe it was Ortiz. No luck there, either. I had her write it, but her penmanship was awful and no help at all. Most of my questions received blank stares.

I started over, "His name is Oteez?"

"Yes."

"And he definitely is in jail?"

"Yes, call me, say come."

"Does he have any other names he uses?"

The blank stare again.

"Do you have a document with his name on it?"

The blank stare.

"Does he use any other last names?"

She looked puzzled, which I thought was an improvement over blank. It was, because she said, "Ross. He have Ross."

It was something, so I looked up Ross and there he was. I couldn't believe it — Otis Ross. I went back to the window and said, "Lady, are you really so dopey that you came to this jail, which has over one thousand people in it, and expected me to know everybody on a first-name basis?"

The blank stare again.

Sometimes there is just a complete failure to connect. A nice black man who had been arrested for DWI the night before was very bewildered when he was released the next morning. I felt sorry for him, as I couldn't seem to get him to understand that he needed to call the towing company to find out where his car was. He was an older man, and he just didn't seem to be able to cope with the situation. Being arrested and spending all night in a loud, crowded, smelly drunk tank can be a very disorienting experience. I called the tow company for him.

"Hi, this is the magistrate. Did you tow a car last night belonging to Thomas Houdon?"

The girl was very nice, with a gentle lilting accent from southwest Virginia's coal country, but said, "Yes, Houdini."

"No, it's Houdon, Thomas," I said. " I'm looking at

his name and it's Houdon."

Still very friendly she says, "No, Houdini, white."

"No, he's a black man. I'm looking right at him."

"I don't know what color he may be sir, but we have his car, a white Houdini. It's one of those new Korean jobs spelled real funny, H-y-u-n-d-a-i."

She was very nice and a bright moment in my day.

One day a Hispanic women was arrested for shoplifting. As opposed to many shoplifters, she at least seemed to be concerned about the situation she found herself to be in. She listened intently as I explained about the arraignment she would have to attend in the morning. Her English was far from perfect, but she was able to understand. I asked her if she had any questions. She said she did in her accented English.

"What's the question?" I asked.

"Do I need a liar with me in the morning?"

How wonderfully perfect, I thought. "No, you don't need a lawyer in the morning. You will later, though, and with that accent you had better look for one with a sense of humor."

The worst English problem I had was not with an arrestee, but with a court employee. In its effort to be politically correct, the court was pursuing a hiring policy which seemed to pay no attention to qualifications or ability. Thus, they hired a nice, young, Puerto Rican junior college student who, honest to God, could not speak English.

People who are arrested and will not be able to make bond must go to an arraignment before a judge the next morning for a review of the bond. These people are interviewed by a pretrial services office about their arrest record, job status, financial condition, ties to the community, marital status etc. The information is made available to the judge at the arraignment. The Puerto Rican student was hired on a part time basis to file these reports alphabetically. It became very obvious to me, quite early on, that he didn't know the alphabet. I was unable to find anything he filed. But I didn't realize the extent of the problem until he came to me one evening and dropped a bombshell with the question, "Escuse me, sir, but can you tell me what ees rubbery?"

I looked at him, somewhat irritated, since I'd been hunting for his filed reports most of the night, and said, "Rubbery? What's rubbery got to do with anything? Why do you want to know that?"

"These mon has bean char wiss rubbery, and I doan know what ees it."

"My God, he means robbery," I blurted.

It got worse. Later on in the evening, his female co-worker came to me with him, looking a little flustered. "Mr. Jasper, could you explain to him what indecent exposure is?"

"Would you like a demonstration, or what?" I snarled.

The final straw came for me when he asked why court was closed on four July. Damn, he was from Puerto Rico, not Papua. Didn't he know anything? I think, in addition to no English, he was just plain dumb. I couldn't believe he was a college student in America, or anywhere else for that matter.

It doesn't bode well for our ever going to the moon again. It does require some book learning to do that, and there doesn't seem to be much of it going on.

The really scary part is that some idiot in the court, apparently dumber yet, had hired him. And who the hell had hired the person who had hired him? How far up the system did you have to go before you ran into a non-idiot? The sad answer is: very high.

What ees rubbery?

Give me a break.

Which brings up the subject of the much-maligned good-old-boy system. Yes, it is abused where it is still strong, and I'll not be going to the trenches to defend it. However, it can work more effectively than it is generally given credit for, especially when viewed in comparison with the supposedly more enlightened affirmative action and other proactive hiring policies in use.

The problem with these more recent policies is responsibility. No one feels responsible or accountable for people newly hired. If a quota is filled or a goal is met, those responsible for the hiring feel that's the end of it. Meeting a quota has become the end task and has displaced the original object of hiring, which was to fill a position with someone best qualified to get the job done. Work capability has been relegated to a secondary role.

At least under the good-old-boy system there is a certain kind of accountability. If Bubba recommends his wife's brother, Billy Bob, for a job, in order not to embarrass himself, Bubba is going to tell whomever he's asking what the brother-in-law's limitations are. And if Billy Bob does get hired, Bubba's going to keep an eye on him, because he is, in the final view of things, his responsibility. If he screws up or turns out to be a complete dolt in the job, they will come to Bubba about it. If he then kicks Billy Bob in the rear a few times, he might straighten out. That's at least some sort of accountability. Of course in a perfect world, the best qualified person should get the job — period. But, what the hell, have you looked closely at your congressman/woman/person lately?

Chapter 19

A Slippery Slope

The battalion I was assigned to in the Army in the early seventies, like a lot of the Army at that time, had an awful racial problem among the blacks, whites, and Hispanics. Two soldiers in one year were murdered in racial fights and several were put in the hospital. I was there for two years, and when I left, the situation was no better. The battalion executive officer, a very impressive major, summed it up in a conversation we had upon my leaving, "The situation will never get better unless we can talk about it. But even to bring up the topic means a risk of being called racist by somebody and even a hint of such an accusation on your record means the end of your career. So everyone wrings his hands, covers his head and lays low. Your career survives but the Army goes to hell."

I'm afraid the court system is not a lot different. A very few malcontents, with their posturing and threats of lawsuits, hold the majority hostage. The whole court system suffers, but those in positions to do anything about it are also those with the most to lose. They are afraid to initiate any review or dialogue, and they thus become part of the problem.

However, in the magistrate's office, with its irreverent attitudes, such subjects are freely discussed. We're already in the basement of the jail. What's to lose? We may not solve any of the problems, but we sure do make a lot of people mighty uncomfortable.

As I've said before, the nature of the job is to inquire, question, be skeptical. When a grossly unqualified person is hired or promoted to a supervisory position, everyone suffers, especially those who rely on the courts for justice and impartiality. When people who have their own agendas to promote are allowed into the system solely to promote those agendas, someone should stand up and shout, "Wrong!"

Trust the magistrates to do just that. For the most part, their proddings of the powers that be have been losing propositions, but the attitude prevails that somebody needs to speak up. Our office has suffered through the years for that attitude. When people are kissing ass, mouthing the latest politically correct platitudes or spouting the party line, they don't take kindly to having their game exposed. We get a black eye for doing it, but as far as we're concerned it's just taking the realistic view of things. Lawbreakers should be gotten off the streets regardless of race, color, creed, or national original. Law abiders should be protected from the lawbreakers, also regardless of race, color, creed, etc. Seems pretty straightforward from our office.

Even though I'm part of the court system, the police have got it right, the courts have got it wrong. In spite of policing having become incredibly more complicated in hundreds of different ways, the police have, commendably, wavered very little from their essential mission: keep the peace, protect the citizens, apprehend the law breakers.

The criminal court system, however, has gone woefully astray. Criminal courts around the world have, for the last few thousand years, existed solely to determine guilt or innocence and to punish the guilty. It really is no more complicated than that. Laws were to protect society from those who were a danger to society. Laws were passed and enforced by the people to protect themselves. Somehow, in this country a least, in the last twenty or thirty years, we have lost our way.

The law, which we have relied upon in the past to protect the innocent, has been subverted and turned on its head, and serves all too frequently now to protect the guilty. It is a very, very dangerous path we are currently following. I see very real evidence of that every day.

Victims of crimes ask me skeptically if it's really worth their time to go to court. They want to believe the system works, but are faced with overwhelming evidence that it does not. I want to believe the system works; I'm part of it. Today I have to be more and more creative than ever in explaining to victims and witnesses why it is important that they testify in court. I certainly can't lie about it. I'm as candid as possible. I explain that convictions aren't that hard to get. A meaningful sentence is what is becoming almost impossible to get.

A very recent decision handed down by a female judge on the circuit court is a perfect example of the stupidity that has become epidemic on the bench. Two illegal aliens from El Salvador had been convicted of a particularly brutal rape of a Hispanic girl. This was no date-rape or cry-rape-the-next-morning situation. The girl was assaulted and raped repeatedly by these two thugs. There were no mitigating circumstances. An innocent girl was brutally attacked. She identified them, and they were convicted.

Then came the sentencing. Ten years in prison; an outrageously light sentence! But there's more. All ten years suspended! Had the judge lost her mind completely? Incredibly, there's more still. No parole, no probation. She ordered them simply to return to El Salvador! Having no authority to do that and no means to enforce such an order, the judge, believing her sentence a stiff one, seemed confused when the two rapists could not stop grinning at each other. Their attorneys sat there in wide-eyed wonderment. Two uneducated, common laborers, who barely spoke English, understood the ineptness of her sentence when she didn't. What on earth could this woman have possibly been thinking? It's okay to do your raping in El Salvador? It's almost okay here, too, apparently.

The perpetrators I see every day are more arrogant, more hostile than ever. Their ever-more-outrageous behavior, both inside and out of jail, is met with weak, almost meaningless punishment. They sneer at it, they laugh at it — literally. When they get out, never anymore a very long wait, why not continue the assaults, robberies and thefts? It's easy and, to them, fun. And even if you do get caught, convicted, and sentenced, problematic in itself, you can do the little bit of time you may get, emphasize *may*, playing poker, and watching television.

I recently had the displeasure of dealing with an arrogant, swaggering piece of garbage who has been arrested over fifty times for assaults, robberies, malicious woundings, and attempted rape. I had dealt with him several times before, most notably when he had robbed a seventy-five-year-old blind woman. He is in his mid-thirties and in twenty years of such despicable crimes, up and down the eastern seaboard in five different states, has spent less than one year in jail. He had just been arrested for yet another assault. His words to me were, "F--k you, man. Go ahead, charge me. I'll beat it. Set any bond you want. I'll be out by morning."

He knew it was true, and I knew it was true. How unsettling knowing that there are thousands of his kind as bad and worse strutting around our neighborhoods, shopping centers, and schools. Maybe someday he'll screw up and assault someone who turns out to be a judge. The criminals need to be careful about that. If they accidentally beat up a few judges, things might start to get a little rough on sentencing days.

The slope gets more slippery the more people lose faith in their system of laws. The more that lawbreakers are not punished meaningfully, the more law abiders begin to wonder why they abide by the laws. We're only human. If we see other people repeatedly get over with something, we begin to wonder why we follow the rules. Slowly but surely, society gets uglier, people get meaner. Values drop, morals slip.

Not that long ago there was a very well-defined line between right and wrong. That line has been defaced and smudged into a very wide grey area of moral "maybe." The legal system has to accept its share of responsibility for that. Decisions handed down seem to say, "Nobody is right, nobody is wrong." Everything is a compromise, a plea bargain. It's a destructive trend born out of convenience and lack of will. It easier to compromise than make hard decisions. But if right is not defended and wrong not punished, morality dies. The felony is reduced to a misdemeanor, the misdemeanor becomes a habit, the habit becomes a lifestyle.

Civilized behavior wanes while the lawmakers, courts, and appointed experts ignore the reality and duck the hard decisions. It is not a theoretical problem. We see the evidence every night on the 6 o'clock news.

Chapter 20

Which Side Is Wonderland?

*T*he public lobby at our office is a constant source of tragedy, wonderment, amusement, anger, and even insanity. We see the public display all the aforementioned, and the public often feels they see the same in the magistrates. The window that separates them from us is like Alice's looking glass. But which side is Wonderland? Some days I think my side is the one that makes sense and that everyone on the other side is nuts. Other days I'm not so sure and think maybe I've been in this job too long and have allowed it to distort my view of things. Most days, though, I just roll with the punches — sometimes as a player, always as an observer. Some days I'm amused; some days I'm disgusted.

I have a colleague whose approach is always direct and straight ahead. I have never once in four years heard him raise his voice. When Flynn, who is six feet four inches, wants to make a point, he speaks with intense, quiet conviction.

One evening a wacko came to the window with the intention of posting a cash bond for his friend in jail. The guy was a real squirrel. First he was going to pay the cash, then he changed his mind and bitched about the bond. Then, when he was about to pay the money, he started calling everybody names for arresting his innocent buddy. He finally stood over in the corner of the lobby pouting and staring at us.

Flynn got up after about a minute of the staring and walked slowly out into the lobby and up to the weirdo. In his usual, quiet, even voice he said, "Listen, you, I don't much give a damn whether you post the bond or not. I also don't care whether your buddy ever gets out of jail. But if you're going to just stand here and stare at me and generally act like an a-- hole, I'm going to be forced get a couple of deputies, and we're going to take you out in the parking lot and rip your balls off."

The wacko, looking understandably stunned, considered that possibility, apparently determined it to be likely, posted the bond immediately, said, "Thank you very much," and left hastily by a route that avoided the parking lot. A little bit of straight talk works wonders sometimes.

Flynn had more trouble with the lobby a few weeks later when he looked up from what he was doing to see a tall young man at the window. He told him to wait just a minute and he'd be with him as soon as he finished what he was doing. When he looked up again, the man was gone. Not that unusual, he'd probably be right back. However, when I happened to walk out into the lobby less than a minute later, I saw him lying on the floor under the window. When I went over it was pretty obvious he was dead as a doornail. We called rescue, but they could do nothing. Dead from an overdose of heroin and cocaine.

The medics discovered $1,000 in cash in his shoe, but no I.D. One of the jailors, playing a hunch, went to the holding tank and asked if anybody had a friend on the way with $1,000 to bond him out. One guy said, "Yes. Is he here?"

The deputy took the information and said, "Better call somebody else. He's had a setback."

It turns out the guy was married and when his wife was called to tell her he was being taken to the hospital, before she asked why, she wanted to know where the $1000 was. Nice. Maybe she was part of the reason he was a heavy drug user. I guess jails made him nervous and he needed a hit in the parking lot before coming in. For a while we all called Flynn "Medusa" — one look and you're stone-cold dead. Nor did Flynn appreciate it when I said to him, "That was real considerate of you, Flynn. That guy's got thirty seconds to live, and you tell him to wait a minute."

On another day, I asked a nicely dressed, pleasant-looking woman at the window if I could help her. She said she certainly hoped so as she had been everywhere and, finally, the FBI had advised her that perhaps a magistrate could help.

"I've been harassed by these two people for a considerable time now, and no one seems to be able to help me. I think it's a jurisdictional problem."

She was very well spoken, if a bit tense, but that was understandable. I asked her to go on.

"Well, these two people have been prying into my personal life and they have also been keeping me under surveillance. It's all gotten very stressful, and I just don't know what to do. They have followed me to several different countries."

"Do you know why these people are doing this?"

"No, I don't have the faintest idea."

She had a cloth handkerchief in her hands that she had begun to twist very tightly.

"Do you know who these people are?"

"Oh, yes. I know their names, and I even have a drawing of each of them that I made."

She withdrew from her purse two notebook-sized pieces of paper. The drawings were excellent. Two very sinister-looking characters, indeed. The horns growing out of one's head and the lightning bolts coming from the other's eyes definitely added to the sinister aura. Uh, oh! Gently, I asked, "And their names?"

"Why, Dr. Death and Mr. Ray. The CIA and the FBI are both aware of them. I've written to both agencies frequently about them."

"You wouldn't happen to have the walls of your bedroom covered in tinfoil, would you, ma'am?"

" Why, yes, I do. Have you heard about the ray machine they use too?"

"I have heard about such from other people."

No need to tell her that most of them were in mental hospitals at the moment. I excused myself and called the police to come and take her to the psychiatric center for an evaluation. While I waited, we had a very nice conversation about the pluses and minuses of quilted versus plain tinfoil and whether it was necessary to cover the floor or not for maximum protection.

When the police arrived I said to her, "Ma'am, these officers are going to take you to a specialist who is very familiar with Dr. Death and Mr. Ray and will be very interested to hear your story."

She thanked me effusively for being so understanding and helpful. She was a very nice lady. I knew I'd done the right thing, and I knew she was going to get help. But somehow, as they escorted her out, I felt like a heel.

As is so often the case, in less than five minutes I was to move from a case of tragedy to one of hilarity. After the police had gone, I was back at the window to learn what a large black woman in her mid fifties needed. She said she had been told by another magistrate earlier in the day that if she came down to our office, she would be able to sign some papers and get her eighteen-year-old son out of jail. He had been charged with driving on a suspended license.

I checked and found it to be so and called the jail to tell them to bring Robert Smith to me as I was allowing his mother to sign for him. Dutifully, they brought Robert Smith. He had white hair, white beard, was 68 years old and he himself was white. I went out to the lobby and brought Mrs. Smith in and pointed out Mr. Smith. "I don't suppose that's your son?"

She looked at me in a queer manner, but began to laugh when she saw me begin to laugh. "I just wanted to be sure before I tell the jailors to try again. I don't suppose you want this one instead?"

All she could do was shake her head in mirth,

bless her.

When I called the booking desk about their small error, the deputy said, "You know, when you called over for him, after I pulled his inmate card and saw he was sixty-eight years old, I almost called you back to ask if mom was in a wheelchair or what."

"Next time, pick up the phone; it's a free call. Now, see if you can find a *black* Robert Smith in the Bastille somewhere before his mother gets suspicious that we may not know what we're doing. We don't want the public to lose faith in us."

On Sunday evenings, as sure as sober follows hungover, we get a steady procession of wives in the lobby bailing their husbands out of jail who were arrested Friday night for being drunk and assaulting them. Every one of them, almost without exception, has the same story: He's a good man when he's sober. He only drinks on weekends. The children need him. He's got to go to work in the morning. If he would only stop drinking everything would be wonderful.

I always have a certain amount of sympathy for their situations, especially the Hispanic wives. What can a woman in a foreign country, with children and no education and a poor command of the language, do on her own? Not much. I usually relent and let the husband go. No matter what their problems, they will only get worse if he misses work and loses his job. Everything will go smoothly until next Friday night when we'll do it all again.

When do I as a magistrate finally say, "No. Enough is enough." These beatings get progressively worse, that's a guarantee. If he stays locked up, he can't beat her. But if he loses his job and he's the sole source of income, have I helped her and her children by keeping him in jail? Yes, I have, and no, I haven't. Most of these guys, when they're released, are truly sorry for what they've done and are willing to swear on their mothers' graves never to drink again. But after a week of digging ditches or hauling bricks or some other backbreaking, bone-crushing labor, a few beers with some friends is impossible to pass up. I find it unbearably sad to watch wife and children tearfully crowding around papa, who is also crying, and hugging him when he's released from jail. Only five more days until Friday.

"If the law suppoes that," said Mr. Bundle . . .
"The law is a ass, a idiot."
— Charles Dickens, *Oliver Twist*

Chapter 21

A Rocket Scientist

I was standing at the rear counter by the sally port entrance one evening, trying to mind my own business, when in comes Officer Donaghue with a big grin on her face.

Officer Donaghue is my kind of gal. Most female officers consider their time on the street working car wrecks and wrestling drunks as a temporary rite of passage that they must endure until they can get promoted to a detective's job. Not Donaghue. She's been on sixteen years, all of it on the street, and she still loves it. She's tough, realistic, a little rough at the edges, but she has a heart of gold and a sense of humor.

My all-time favorite story about Donaghue is the night she and her dad went out to have a few drinks celebrating her birthday. They had a few too many, and when the bartender cut them off, Donaghue got a little insulted and a few unkind words were exchanged. The barkeep decided he didn't like Donaghue's attitude and called the police. She and her pop had gone drinking in another county, so when the police showed up, she didn't know them and they didn't know her. If the cops had just asked her to move on, that's exactly what she and pop would have done. But the local gendarme were feeling a little frisky that night and decided to get into Donaghue's face. Donaghue, who "don't take no s--t from nobody," spoke her piece and stood her ground. The details were never clear, but the damnedest fist fight broke out and, after a call for more officers went out, Donaghue and her old man spent the night in the slammer.

Their chief of police was pretty hot. A couple of his officers had black eyes and swollen lips. Donaghue was no slouch with her fists and neither, apparently, was pops. Donaghue's chief was more than hot. So much so it looked for a while that Donaghue's days as a police officer were over. Eventually, she ended up with a boatload of time off without pay and loss of a hard-earned stripe. She had been one of the first female officers on the force, and that probably helped her not end up in the unemployment line.

Tonight Officer Donaghue had answered a complaint about a suspicious man at the train station. She arrived at the station and immediately saw the problem. The man was suspicious because he was standing on the train platform without a stitch of clothing on. He was a plump, grandfatherly sort with white hair and a white beard. *All* of his hair was white, as a matter of fact. His only possession, which he had in his hand, was his driver's license. He had been very cooperative and agreed to sit in the police cruiser while Officer Donaghue tried, with no success, to find his clothes — or any clothes. So here they were in front of me, with her smiling and him smiling and me smiling. What else can one do with a pleasant, naked Santa Claus look alike?

"Mr. Kennedy, your driver's license says you're from Jupiter Beach, Florida."

"That's right." Still smiling.

"What happened to your clothes?" I asked.

"I took them off. It's my constitutional right to not wear clothes."

"But other people have a right of not having to look at your nakedness."

"Possibly so. Nonetheless, I feel my right is unassailable."

By now a jailor had brought a blanket to cover Mr. Kennedy, which he accepted readily enough. I guess he was through with his display of constitutional rights.

"Well, Mr. Kennedy, you will have to go to court on a charge of disturbing the peace, and at that time you can present your claim of right under the constitution to the judge."

"That will be quite satisfactory."

"However, I'm afraid I am going to have to hold you here for a while to give us time to get to know some more about you. We have court interviewers who will talk to you. I need to be sure that you will come to court."

"Oh, rest assured I will. Perhaps I can call my son. I'm visiting him here, you know."

"Actually I didn't know, but that would be helpful for us to talk with him."

The old boy positively beamed when talking about his son, so I asked him, "What does your son do?"

"He's an aeronautical engineer with NASA at Langley Air Force Base in Maryland."

"And what about you? Are you retired?"

"Oh no, I'm a research scientist with NASA at Cape Canaveral."

"Been under a little stress lately?" I asked lightly.

"Why, yes. As a matter of fact, we have been having some setbacks in our particular project lately. Why do you ask?"

"No particular reason. Just idle curiosity, I guess. You go with the officer over to the jail now, and we'll talk to your son."

When officer Donaghue returned, she was still amused. "How many times in the past have I brought before you some dumbass who has done some incredibly stupid thing to get arrested and I've said, 'Well, Mr. Jasper, I got me another rocket scientist here.'"

"It's one of your favorite sayings, Officer Donaghue."

"It took me sixteen years, but I finally arrested a real one, and naked at that."

"Life is sweet, Officer Donaghue. Now get out of here while I go call the son to come and pick up dad."

Another old boy from Florida came to our attention one night when one of the deputies stopped an elderly man driving his camper truck erratically and aimlessly through the courthouse parking lot. He didn't know who he was or where he was going. He did remember that he and his wife had left Florida a few days ago and the last he had seen of her was near Richmond somewhere; how long ago, he wasn't sure. He didn't have any identification on him, but the Florida license tag came back registered to a name he thought sounded familiar. He did know that he and his wife lived in Florida, but every spring they packed up and drove to New York to stay with their son for the summer. He couldn't remember the name of the town.

Somehow, the old fellow's case became my responsibility. He was very charming and most anxious to please. That was somewhat of a problem, however, because he would agree with any suggestion I made. And that was what I was reduced to, making suggestions. He just couldn't answer any direct questions about anything. His memory had deserted him. In trying to establish his route, I suggested various roads he may have taken. He agreed to all of them. He thought they all sounded familiar.

I was becoming extremely worried about his wife. I was afraid she may have been injured and the image of a poor old lady lying beside the road somewhere haunted me. He just couldn't remember anything, even when I tacitly suggested the possibility of such a thing to him in hopes of jogging his memory.

I got the police and their remarkable communications system involved. There were no reports of missing persons fitting our friend's description between Florida and Virginia. The Florida police went by the address and had not been able to add anything to what we knew. Nobody was home, and the neighbors said that they had left for New York. Four hours had gone by, and we were nowhere.

Then the deputy came in and reported he had been going through the camper and had discovered an address book. In the book was a name and phone number in New York which just might be the son's. I called, and, hallelujah, it was and we were part way home.

The wife was still my main worry. The son told us that his father had called before leaving Florida two days ago. He had not heard from them since, but that was not unusual. He did tell us that his mother was driving a car while the father drove the camper. I didn't know if that made me feel better or worse. The son said he'd get the first flight out and be there as soon as he could. We were out of options as to what else to do about the wife. The son gave a description of the car, and the police sent a lookout up and down the Atlantic coast. All we could do was wait.

After two hours we got good news, but not from where we expected. The son called and told us that mom had just pulled into the driveway, safe and sound.

Her story was a sequence of wrong assumptions. They stopped for the night near Richmond and were in the motel room preparing to go out for dinner. When she came out of the shower, he was gone. She assumed he would be right back. After he didn't show, she went out to the parking lot thinking he was in the camper. It was gone. Still thinking he would be back soon, she waited. After an hour, she went to the police. For some reason I never understood, they told her there was nothing they could do. And they were true to their word. They did nothing. Not even a teletype entry. She pretty much got the brush-off.

She went back to the motel, waited around for a few hours, and then decided that he must have driven on to New York ahead of her. Not knowing anybody in Richmond and having gotten no help from the police, she decided to drive on also.

I talked to the son a few days later and he said his father remembered little of that day. He had the family doctor doing some tests. Everybody was doing okay, and he assured me there would be no more driving between New York and Florida. It was the happy ending we had hoped for but, in our line of work, frequently don't get.

"Every peasant has a lawyer inside of him,
just as every lawyer, no matter how urbane he may be,
carries a peasant within himself."
— Miguel de Unamuno

Chapter 22

Combat Boots and a Mini-skirt

I don't understand the statistical significance in that some nights, many of the cases I handle have a melancholy tinge to them, and then other nights, most cases keep me smiling. Perhaps it's something going on only in my mind. Whatever the reason, I welcome the humor whenever it arrives.

One midnight, a drunk came in wearing a t-shirt that read, "Instant a--hole, just add beer." I liked that, and it was certainly true in his case.

A DWI said to me, "If you're not supposed to drink and drive, how come bars got parking lots?"

I didn't like that much. But his question caught me so off guard I didn't have an answer either.

One particular drunk seemed to be having an on-going contest of wills with the arresting officer. When the cop hauled him in, I noticed the drunk had a cut on his chin that was dripping blood. "What happened to him?" I asked.

"Oh, Mr. Hotshot here thought he would show his ignorance in front of his friends by assaulting my fist with his chin."

"Police brutality?"

"No doubt."

From the drunk, "I'm not drunsh. I only ha' two beersh. I gotta pee."

I was ten feet away, and the smell of alcohol was overpowering.

He looked at me through glassy eyes and slurred, "Jesch you wait. Inna couple hours Rosh Perot and Roosh Limbaugh will be here to gesch me."

The cop rolled his eyes and said, "Gimme your name, will ya."

To which the drunk slurred, "Wassa matter, you don't like yours?"

The cop looked at me, "I don't need this. All I wanted was a cup of f--kin' coffee and a chili dog at 7-Eleven, which I never got. Instead, I get this a--hole who's s--tface drunk and wants to show off to his buddies by taking a swing at me when I get out of the cruiser. Jesus, I don't even know where he came from. Lucky for me he's so drunk he misses by a mile. I pop him once, and down he goes like a ton of s--t."

"And if you would raise your right hand and swear to me that your graphic testimony is, in fact, the truth and nothing but the truth, officer."

"You bet."

From the drunk, "Don't I get to say anything?"

"What would you like to say?"

"I gotta pee."

"Duly noted."

Once more from the drunk, "Ossifer, you sure are an ugly motherf--ker."

"Well, Mr. whatever your name is, I guess the jailors will think we're brothers, then, when they see us."

Point, counterpoint. Maybe not intellectual debate, but it does have its moments.

About that time the police brought in a young girl who was wearing dark sunglasses, even though it was midnight. When I looked inquisitively at the officer, he shrugged and said, "When you're cool, the sun always shines."

The drunk was sitting next to where the police had deposited the girl on the bench. He kept staring closely at her, and she kept staring straight ahead, pointedly ignoring him. As the officer said, she was cool, real cool. What apparently was fascinating the drunk was a diamond stud the girl had inserted through the side of her nostril. Obviously, the drunk had never seen such a thing.

She finally turned her head to him and hissed, "You got a problem, man?"

Undeterred, he continued to stare as if she were not there, only the diamond. Then very clearly he asked, "Is that a diamond booger in your nose?"

Her coolness had been dealt a death blow.

Next in was Officer Cox, who had arrested a self-appointed, very important drunk who was demanding his badge number, name, superiors, authority to arrest him, etc. He was plopped down on the other side of the first drunk. Since the diamond girl was definitely not even acknowledging the existence of Drunk #1 now, he shifted his attention to Mr. Important

Drunk, who was ranting and raving about how he would have the officer's job and how he knew important people. Since Mr. Perot and Mr. Limbaugh would soon be down to get our first drunk, he was not impressed with Mr. Important Drunk — in the least. He listened intently, though, until Mr. Important Drunk noticed he had an audience, whereupon he turned to the first drunk and demanded, "Have you also been illegally deprived of your liberty by these Gestapo goons?"

The question seemed to startle the first drunk, but he considered it and replied slowly, "I don't think so. I'm just drunk."

I thought that was interesting when just moments before he had been claiming to have drunk just two beers. Having not received anything like the response he wanted, Mr. Important Drunk demanded, once again in a loud voice, the officer's name.

Hoping to shut him up for a few moments, Officer Cox turned and said, "Cox, okay? My name will be on the warrant."

To which Mr. Important Drunk demanded, "Is that spelled the normal way?"

To which our now more mellowed first drunk marveled, "I sure hope he doesn't spell it any other way."

And if things were not confusing enough, in came another officer with a DWI with the best-looking pair of legs that I'd seen in many a year. Black fishnet stockings, black leather miniskirt, expensive silk blouse, high proud bust, long blond hair. Everyone became quiet. There were just two minor problems — the combat boots and the black moustache. She (?) sat down on the bench next to our man still waiting for

Rush and Ross. Legs turned to him and in a deep baritone said, "How ya doin', man?"

I don't know what amazed me more. What good-looking legs he had, even in combat boots, or the moustache and five o'clock shadow offset by expertly applied lipstick. If I was amazed, the drunk he was sitting next to looked ready to go into shock.

The cop, having yet to get a name from him, saw his opportunity and drew the drunk aside and up close to him and whispered, "If you don't give me your name, then you'll go into the jail as a John Doe, and I'll ask the jailors to make sure you share a cell with tutti-frutti there. What's it going to be, a name or a wide-awake night together with Goldilocks ?"

At last, with no more hesitation, a name was produced, warrant written, off to jail 'til morning.

Which brought us to Mr. Important Drunk. A bombastic, loudmouthed, arrogant drunk always draws a crowd of kibitzer-jailors and magistrates. The following was pretty typical.

"Let go of me, you cretin cop, or I'll charge you with assault and false arrest."

"Yeh, yeh. Now this here's the magistrate, so stop acting like an a--hole 'cause he decides when you're getting out of here."

"How dare you call me an a--hole."

"Excuse me all to hell, Mr. A--hole."

The drunk looks at me, "You don't know who you're dealing with."

I look at him, "A drunk, perhaps?"

"I've had two glasses of white wine. I'm certainly not drunk. You can't judge me like that."

"But that's exactly what they pay me to do."

"You are a public servant. I pay your salary."

From a deputy, "Say, I've been looking for you. How the hell come you only gave me a two-percent raise this year? I've got a wife and two kids to feed."

That slowed down Mr. Important Drunk for a second, but just for a second. "I have a very important position on Capitol Hill."

From another kibitzer, "I'll bet. Probably face down and butt up."

Pointedly ignoring that, he looked me over with obvious distaste, "It is impossible that someone in such an obviously cheap sports coat has the authority to put me in jail. What did you pay for that, twenty-five dollars?"

That brought whistles and catcalls from everyone.

"I'm sorry if my sartorial selection offends you, and since I have serious doubts in my mind that you would be able to find time in your busy and important life to attend your trial here, I am, regrettably, forced to set your bond at the equivalent of one hundred sports coats. Deputy, take the gentlemen to the fitting room for his exclusive jail garb selection."

It was time to talk to Goldilocks. Such cross-dressing is not as rare as one would think — or wish. I have dealt with several over the last twelve years, and it just doesn't lead anywhere to try and pursue a line of questioning about why the particular person you're talking to dresses that way. Like as not the most you'll ever get to a direct question of, "Why do you dress that way?" is a shrug of the shoulders.

I have never been very persistent about it, anyway. It's not illegal, and I don't really want to know why. Goldilocks was a DWI and quite pleasant. He was a plumber and had been working for the same plumbing firm for twenty years. There was absolutely nothing effeminate in his mannerism or speech at all. He even walked like a plumber as opposed to a plumberette, I guess. He was fifty-four years old and was driving back from a party in Charlottesville. He was wearing boots instead of the "normal" high heels because it was easier to drive his 3/4-ton, stick-shift pickup with boots. It must have been quite a party.

I asked him, "Most people don't wear lipstick with a moustache?"

"Yes, that's true," he replied quite evenly in his deep voice.

"Have you ever been arrested before?"

"No."

"It's December. Don't your, ah, essentials get cold in a miniskirt?"

"Not really."

As I said, you just never get very far with these guys. There was no doubt in my mind that he would be in court when he was supposed to and that he was probably a damned good plumber, too. But as my wife said one night after listening to me describe a weekend of cross-dressing plumbers, drunk painters, and pot puffing electricians, "The next time we get any work done on this house, I'm going to find a company that hires only retired nuns."

"Oaths are but words, and words but wind."
— Samuel Butler

Chapter 23

Battling Bridesmaids

*O*ne evening I had a case which will not be featured in *Brides Magazine*. At the public window, several very elegantly dressed, but distraught people in their twenties had congregated. It seemed two of their friends, both young ladies, had been arrested by the police and were on their way to see me.

"Why were they arrested?" I asked the group.

"They got into a fight at the rehearsal dinner," one girl quietly replied.

"You mean like in 'wedding rehearsal' dinner?"

"Yes," replied the very woebegone bride to be.

"How did the police get involved?"

"We couldn't get them to stop fighting, and the hotel manager called the police," she said with tears in her eyes.

I had the young woman come into the office and tell me her tale. She had two, very dear high school friends whom she wanted to be in her wedding. One now lived in California the other in Colorado. The problem was that the two had been bitter enemies since high school. At one time they had been friends, but a rivalry over a boyfriend changed that forever. The boyfriend shamelessly played one against the other until the rivalry had festered into resentment, then bitterness and, eventually, hatred. There was never a reconciliation between the two. In spite of all that, the bride was determined to have her two friends share in her joy and help celebrate her nuptials. As most anyone could have predicted — big mistake.

Neither wanted to be anywhere near the other, but the bride begged and pleaded and, reluctantly, they agreed. They had not seen each other for eight years, which the bride thought would have been enough time for feelings to have cooled. But, instead, nothing had cooled, and the feud was simply picked up again and continued when they were brought together in Virginia. There was sniping and minor ambushes by both, but the bride persisted in believing she could keep it under control. It was, after all, her glorious moment and surely her two best friends wouldn't allow themselves to ruin that.

It all came to a head at the rehearsal dinner, in spite of the bride's best efforts. A look led to a stare, a stare to a nudge and the fight was finally on. And what a fight it was. Roundhouse swings, bites, kicks, punches, all in a beautifully decorated, private dining room at an expensive hotel. No one could stop them, and finally the manager called the police when the combatants began to break up the crystal, plates and table centerpieces.

When the police arrived, they were still going at

it, and it took two burly cops to finally separate them as the rest of the wedding party cowered at the other end of the room, trying to stay out of the way of flying debris from the battle.

As she finished her story, the police arrived with the two combatants. What a shambles. Beautiful gowns in tatters, stockings torn, hair in disarray, hands in cuffs, and still trying to fight each other! Upon seeing them, the bride burst into tears, probably for the twentieth time that night. The two cops left the ladies in the able hands of the jailors for safe keeping and came into the office.

"Well, Mr. Jasper, what do you want to do?" one smiled at me innocently. He was quite content that it was my problem.

I gave him a dirty look. "Does anyone want to press charges? How about the hotel manager?"

"Not him. As long as he gets the damages paid for."

The bride sighed as she thought about that bill.

"But," smiled the cop, "the two ladies both want to press assault charges against each other."

That elicited a sigh from me. One from California, one from Colorado. No one was going to come back to court, although from experience I knew they both would swear up and down that they would fight the hounds of hell if need be to get back — and then no one would show. Charging anybody would be pointless, since neither of them, despite their enthusiasm, had inflicted any lasting damage on the other. They managed to break up a lot of things, but fortunately not each other.

I said to the bride, "I presume you and your fiancee will be taking care of the damages at the hotel?"

To which she nodded yes.

"If I charge anybody here I'll have to put that

person in jail under a bond."

The bride's eyes got wide in alarm as she stammered, "If I have to bond someone out of jail it will be with the money we've saved for our honeymoon." Then she really began to bawl. "I don't want to miss our honeymoon. Oh, God. How could things have gone so wrong?"

For the one hundredth time in my career as a magistrate, I thought, Damn, what a mess. Now what? Since everybody in this whole fiasco was acting as if rational thinking was a forbidden exercise, I decided that a direct, "I'm in charge, you're not," approach would work best.

I had the jailors set both women down together in an interview room after making it very clear that if they so much as raised their voices to each other or me they would both find themselves in solitary confinement. I also brought in both cops and two of the biggest, meanest looking female jailors I could find. Out of earshot, I quietly said to the jailors that hard, intense, cold stares at the two women would be appropriate.

I chose a small interview room with the two sitting down across from me while I had the cops and jailors stand on either side of them. Things were extremely tight. Perfect, I thought. They looked small, crowded and, most important, intimidated. They weren't exactly holding each other's hands, especially with cuffs on, but as the jailors stared and the cops' leather creaked loudly whenever they moved, the two did slide, probably unconsciously and almost imperceptibly, closer to each other.

I looked exasperated and began, "I'm appalled.

Two grown women acting like sixth graders. No, that's insulting to sixth graders. The most important time in your friend's life and you two have turned it into a B-grade movie farce. Very considerate of both of you. I wouldn't hesitate for a minute to lock both of you up except for your friend out there crying her eyes out. If it wasn't for the fact that she would use her honeymoon money to bail you out of jail, that's exactly where I'd put you. In return for loyalty like that you drag her wedding plans in the mud. Wonderful. And now I hear you want warrants against each other. Were you going to subpoena the bride so she could be further humiliated and laughed at in court testifying about the infamous rehearsal dinner free for all? I would have been hard pressed to make up a story as outlandish as this."

They were looking utterly miserable, which was encouraging.

"I'm going to save both of you considerable embarrassment by refusing to even consider assault warrants."

They didn't look too disappointed about that as they warily eyed the imposing police presence. I went out and informed the bride of my decision. The wedding party heaved a sigh of relief. I gave them ten minutes to make plans for the imminent release and separation of the two hellcats, since I didn't trust either of them not to take a swing as soon as they were in the parking lot. It was only after they left that I realized that I had not allowed either of them to say even one word. I didn't solve their problems nor did I settle any feuds with the wisdom of Solomon that night, but they didn't come back before the end of my shift and that's a win in my view.

"The ethical distinction between lying to a jury and pulling the wool over its eyes is surely a fine one."
— Phillip Johnson

Chapter 24

Just Bizarre

It was a 2-1 split decision. Flynn said, "Man." Joan, my other partner, said, "Woman." I tried to not vote since I was stumped. That was not allowed, so, without a lot of conviction, I voted "woman," not from anything empirical, just a guess.

The subject had been brought in from another station and taken to the booking desk. The three of us lined up like crows on a fence as we watched the booking process from our office on the other side of the holding area leading to the booking desk. Would the subject be led farther back into the men's area or be brought back out to the elevator for the trip up to the women's area? At six feet three inches, about two hundred and fifty pounds, and a lot of fat, it could go either way. I strained to hear a voice as she/he answered questions put to him/her by the booking deputies. Deep, but nothing conclusive.

A photograph was taken and apparently a decision made, as she was being led this way to the elevator and the female block. The three of us watched silently.

"At the risk of appearing insensitive," I ventured, "That was one ugly woman"

A deputy nearby said, "The issue is still in doubt. She claims female but we're taking her upstairs for a female deputy to take a close, unclothed look."

Joan shuddered and said, "There ain't enough money in this jail for me to be the one."

"The deputy gets to keep her clothes on, don't you understand?" It earned me a punch in the arm.

"I don't date women who can bench press me," was my final contribution.

I began to think about some of the more bizarre-looking people who came before me in the past. One Halloween, I listened to testimony from a woman who had appeared decked out in a very elaborate and re-alistic-looking witches' costume (light green skin, big wart on her nose, scraggly hair) about the need for a mental detention for her husband. He, in the middle of a Halloween party, decided it was time again to go around the bend. It was not his first such excursion.

I agreed to issue the detention order. What kept running through my mind as I sat there listening was, "I don't think we're in Kansas anymore, Toto." She even had on a tall, pointed witch's hat, which neither of us thought to remove, throughout the whole hearing.

Then there was the one-legged drunk. He had been found by the side of the road, near the bus station, passed out with an empty bottle of wine beside him. The police department, in a medium-size town down-state, had enough of him and bought a bus ticket one night after his one millionth drunk-in-public charge. He still had the ticket in his pocket.

No doubt our police would return the favor one day, if not with this drunk then at least one of equal value. It doesn't happen a lot, nor nearly as much as it used to. After the same drunk gets arrested every night for several weeks, even my patience gets a little thin — and I don't have to wrestle with them or get puked on or have them defecate in my car. So it's no wonder that, occasionally, the hat gets passed at roll call and a semiconscious drunk finds himself on the big dog headed out of town that night.

It became obvious pretty quickly why this drunk had earned a ticket out of town. He was one mean son of a bitch. Once he was roused enough to realize he was being arrested by a female cop, he bellowed and screamed that he wasn't gonna be arrested by no homosexual cop. He kept trying to slug the cop with his crutch and, one legged or not, he did his best to kick anyone who came within range. Mostly, though, he just fell on his ass every time he tried.

When they brought him to me, he sat on the floor trying to trip anyone who came near by sticking out his one foot. He was filthy, had sores, and smelled worse then buzzard puke. As the jailors led him away, he tried one more feeble kick and would have fallen on his ass again if they hadn't been holding him up. It prompted one of the jailors to yell out, "Better get some leg irons on this guy!"

The arresting cop looked at me and said, "Phew, I thought *we* had a mean sense of humor."

"Ah," I said warmly, " I'd put the jailors up against *anybody* for low blows and tasteless humor." I knew them to be an organization with a lot of pride.

"Lost is our old simplicity of times,
The world abounds with laws and teems with crimes."
— Anonymous

Chapter 25

Lassie, Come Home

It was weird, sick, strange, outrageous. The newspaper reporters, although fascinated with it, couldn't get their editors to publish a story on it. It was the damnedest case I ever handled. As happens frequently, it began with a solemn-looking officer coming into the office with, "Whew, do I have a can of worms for you, sir."

If it was a busy day, it was time to look busier in hopes he'd unburden himself on somebody else. But if it was a slow day, such cases made the time go by. It was a slow day so I put the officer under oath, and we were off.

"First of all, animal control and the police department have been passing this case back and forth for two weeks. The dog owner keeps demanding action, and our chief decided we would do it. Just my s--tty luck to be at the wrong place and wrong time. I can't believe I gotta go to court and testify about this s--t."

He did look pretty miserable about it, I had to admit. This must be a real doozy.

"I guess we first got the call from this guy about his dog. But the communications center contacted animal control. Animal control went out and talked to the guy because I think they originally didn't believe what the guy was saying. Well, after they checked it out a little bit, they dropped it like a hot potato, and them and the police department passed the buck back and forth like I said, until the chief got involved. Who I pissed off, I don't know, but it's my case now."

I couldn't even begin to imagine what this was going to be.

"So I go out and talk to this guy. He tells me he uses this day laborer off and on to do yard work around his house. Been using him for a couple years. He says he comes home one afternoon and when he comes in the front door he hears his dog whining and growling in the garage. At first he thinks, no big deal. The dog's cornered a squirrel maybe. But the whining doesn't sound right. Almost like the dog's hurting. So he goes to the door to the garage and opens it."

Here the officer has to stop for a moment. He looks at me and shakes his head.

"Fer Chrissake, there's the handyman humping away on Lassie. He's got the damned dog on it's back, all four paws in the air and this pervert, weirdo pumping up and down, sir." The cop pauses again, looking miserable. "Jesus H. Christ, how am I going to testify in court about this s--t?"

I could sympathize with the man, although it didn't seem like the dog owner was going to have a fun time testifying either. Of course, that was a cakewalk compared to the handyman's day in court. I shuddered at the thought. Ever helpful, I asked, "Are you going to subpoena the dog?"

I could see the court transcript.

"Now, Miss Lassie, how would you describe this terrible experience?"

"Ruff! Ruff!"

The officer managed a weak smile.

I wrote the warrant charging copulation with an animal, and the officer went off glumly to make the arrest. He didn't consider this case a career-advancing opportunity and was already tiring of the perverted humor at the station directed at him. I obviously had not assuaged his feelings, either.

Later in the day when the felon was brought in, he immediately wanted to explain himself. I immediately told him I did not want to hear it, which I wholeheartedly didn't. I set bond and turned him over to the jailors.

Apparently, he'd been in jail before, because the booking officer greeted him. "Leonard, you've been in here a few times before. Too much to drink now and again, a little larceny here and there. But I don't know what to say about this one. You've expanded your field of interest. Lordy, lordy, I don't know whether to call the S.P.C.A. or Friends of the Animals."

Leonard attracted a crowd. Word of this *cause célèbre* had flashed throughout the jail almost instantaneously, and everybody wanted a look at the "dog man." As he was led off to a cell, a chorus of barking "dogged" him down the hallway.

Leonard was duly convicted in spite of a spirited

defense by his court-appointed lawyer. Not a case on which to build a legal reputation or be considered for partnership. I'm sure several lawyers used many dodges to avoid the case; still, someone had to eventually get stuck. I believe the defense was a convoluted tale of tripping over the dog and falling while the dog rolled over and, "Whoops!" But, apparently, the fact that Leonard had his pants around his ankles could not be explained away completely, among other problems. It must have been quite a day in court.

The officer did pay me back for my earlier dig at him. After court he came to tell me the sentence, "One hundred hours of community service at the dog pound," he told me, very seriously. I looked at him in amazement and started to ask who was going to keep an eye on Leonard, when the cop broke into a grin and growled, "Gotcha!" Leonard actually got a few months in jail and alcoholism counseling.

Chapter 26

Dumbasses

*M*ost crooks are just plain stupid. The so-called master criminal, who occasionally pops up in the newspapers, is called that only because he has an I.Q. approaching his body temperature; whereas most crooks who, whether due to genes, drugs, or alcohol, can't consistently get two plus two to equal the vast sum of four.

I just recently handled an awful case where a low-life scum sneaked into an old folks' home and raped a seventy-year-old lady. He threatened to come back unless she wrote him a blank check for $50. He then took it to her bank where he carefully filled in his name, showed proper identification, and got the cash. When the lady got her monthly bank statement and saw the check, she called the police. There, along with his name, was his social security number entered on the back of the check by the teller. The police ran the information, got an address, went by his house, knocked on the door, and dragged the piece of garbage off to jail.

Prostitutes fall into the just-plain-stupid category, too. In twelve years I have yet to see even one prostitute who did not give me the creeps. They have so far, without one exception, been disease-ridden, drug-infested horror shows. They smell bad and look awful. Most of them will probably be dead within a few years from drugs, disease or a knifing. I used to try and talk some sense into them, but all I ever got back was abuse or resignation. It's depressing and frustrating dealing with them. They just don't give a damn about themselves or anybody else.

One day, the police arrested a man because an adjoining county had sent a teletype stating they had a warrant for him. I could not get it through his thick head what was going on. He was convinced that, since he did not live in that county, they couldn't have a warrant for him. He agreed that he had been there many times and had maybe even gotten into some trouble over there. But he could not understand how they had any authority to issue arrest warrants for him since he didn't live there.

I finally gave up trying to explain it, telling him he was just going to have to trust me on this one — they had the authority to write it, and I had the authority to put him in jail. He pondered that line of reasoning, but was still shaking his head as he went into jail. Life just wasn't fair.

The dumbest question asked by those in the stupid-crook category is that asked by all drug dealers when there is a suspicion in their minds that the guy they're getting ready to sell to is an undercover cop. "You ain't the police, is you? You not five-oh are you man?"

I can't imagine what these guys think asking the question is supposed to accomplish. What do they expect the cop to say? "Aw s--t, man, why'd you have to ask me that? Yeah, you're right, I'm the fuzz. Damn, man why'd you have to go and do that? Now I got to go back to the station and tell the captain you found me out. Man, my day's ruined."

A particularly dangerous combination of stupidity and drugs occurred one night when an unemployed crackhead sat thinking about his life and how much he really thought it sucked and how much he actually hated life and his girlfriend, too. He liked getting high, but he sure was tired of her bitching at him about it. He'd like to get high even more but the stuff was getting too damned expensive. Life was sure getting to be a drag. He needed money for a good time, but he damned sure wasn't going to get a job. That was for chumps. Couldn't seem to hit the damned lotto number, either. S--t, guess he'd have to do his own lotto. 7-Eleven had gotten enough of his money playing that. It was time to get some back. Drugs can do some real strange things to your mind.

Every person living in the U.S.A. who has ever handed a 7-Eleven clerk a $20 bill knows the problems that causes. It seems they are not allowed to keep more than $3 in the drawer at one time. Every person, it seems, but *one* knows that. Our crackhead weirdo was the one. He got his gun and set out to seek his fortune.

He was mightily perturbed after the first 7-Eleven robbery netted only $15. He headed for the second one. Maybe he'd hit the jackpot there. But they only had $17. S--t!

After the third 7-Eleven got robbed that night on Route 1, the police department had this one figured out. When our crackhead walked out after robbing the fourth 7-Eleven, he was facing enough weaponry to kill him at least 10,000 times over. That was enough to sharply focus even his drug-addled mind. Gun in hand, he considered the multitude of muzzles pointed at him and decided that his take of $57 was not worth dying for. He laid the gun down slowly and put his hands up. At the bail hearing, his only question to me was "Hey, man, how many times does four go into fifty-seven?"

Sheer, dumb-assed stupidity may have been elevated to new heights by three twenty-year-olds standing in the middle of the street one night. A female officer rounded the corner in her cruiser and about ran off the road at the sight presented to her. Three across they stood, facing her, absolutely buck naked waving their penises in unison, back and forth, as if in a chorus line. Not unlike The Rockettes, in a rather perverted way.

Our trusty officer admitted to me later that she was so dumbfounded that, after coming to a quick stop, she just sat there with her mouth hanging open in amazement as the bump-and-grind routine continued.

After an undetermined amount of time, she regained her composure and, no doubt with a certain amount of mischievous glee, made her police presence known by turning on her siren and emergency lights. Their response was, no doubt, most satisfying to the officer. After an initial frenzied, unintended Three

Stooges act of running into each other several times in panic, the officer reported that they "high tailed" it out of there in a flurry of elbows and rear ends. As she followed them with her headlights and spotlights, they headed for the door of the nearest house, which failed to yield to their furious attempts at entry. Seems as if the door was locked and nobody had thought to bring a key. Where they would have kept such a key is unknown. How they had managed to allow themselves to get locked out is also unknown. But then how can you explain anything about three guys who thought it would be a fun lark to stand in the street and wave their genitalia at the motoring public?

Our officer on the scene approached the three, standing against the wall in various ineffectual covering poses, and in yet another mischievous dig asked, "Anybody got any identification on them?" to which she got various mumbles and stammers. Everybody had been drinking, but the officer was surprised that nobody was even near to being drunk.

Realizing that to arrest all three and take them to jail stark naked would make her the butt of enough jokes and ribbing from the jailors to last her a lifetime, the officer allowed one to crawl through an open window (that in itself, she said, was worth the price of admission) and open the door. She determined who everybody was and that, even though these guys were probably the three dopiest people she had ever met, they hadn't been acting with malice.

It was more of a dare, a double dare, a triple dare. No explanation would ever be really adequate. She gave them each a summons for public lewdness and the assurance that the matter could probably be handled quietly in a pretrial agreement with the commonwealth's attorney. She warned them though that if she had to come and find them, if they were to miss court, then she would be compelled to prosecute in open court. If they were embarrassed now when *she* was the only witness, they didn't know the meaning of the word until she testified, in detail, in a crowded court room about their disgraceful behavior tonight. She would be sure to omit absolutely nothing.

They assured her repeatedly that they would show up whenever and wherever directed. They did show as directed and, I believe, spent several weekends gathering trash along the roads, fully clothed.

Some stunts are even *more* than stupid. I'm not sure what dimension that puts them in, but one occasionally hears about the bank robber who writes the holdup note on the back of his gas bill or the burglar who drops his wallet inside the window sill. I used to hear such stories and wonder if people were really that dumb? Or was it just press hype to sell newspapers or attract viewers during sweeps week? Alas, for the human race (we all share the same gene pool), but fortunately for the police, people *are* that dumb.

A young man came into a shoe store one day looking for a job. He was pleasant, clean cut, and conservatively dressed. The manager gave him an employment application and asked him to bring it back the next day at 3:00 p.m. when he would have the time to sit down with him. Precisely at 3:00 p.m. the next day he returned, impressing the manager, who

was finishing with a customer. He took the application and told him to look around the store for a few
minutes and then they would be able to go into his
office. When the sale was done, he glanced over the
application and liked what he saw. Just finished high
school, planning on going to the community college
in the fall, wanted the job to help pay tuition. He
looked up, about to invite what he thought was his
soon-to-be new employee into the office, and saw him
nonchalantly put a pair of shoes under his jacket
and start for the exit.

He shouted, "Hey, what are you doing?" and the
no longer about-to-be-new employee bolted for the door
and streaked down the sidewalk.

The kid could have been a track star because by
the time the manager got out the door, he was around
the corner and gone. Mad as hell, the manager
walked back into the store and then realized he still
had the employment application in his hand. Must
be bogus, he thought. He had to begrudgingly admit
it was a pretty good scam. He'd sure been taken in.
Kind of complicated for one pair of shoes, though.
He almost threw it away, but figured the police would
like to see it. A pretty good scam, all right.

While he was waiting for the police, another young
man, also clean cut and nicely dressed, came in the
store and asked if his cousin was still there. As the
manager wondered about this latest development, the
police arrived and, on his urgent request, latched onto
the new arrival.

As it turned out, he had no idea what had happened and, yes, the applicant was his cousin and, yes,
he had ridden with him to the job interview and, yes,

the information on the application was correct.

The police went by the address on the form and duly arrested the young miscreant, already wearing his new pair of shoes.

His explanation? He had decided that he probably wasn't going to get the job (why he had decided that, he couldn't say) and figured the time he'd spent filling out the application was worth a pair of shoes. And what about that job application he had left behind? Well, he sort of forgot about that.

This kid wasn't the only criminal around town. Somebody down at the community college had committed a fraud by taking his money with the pretense that it could lead to a diploma. Even with today's lowered standards, it plain wasn't doable.

Chapter 27

A Jerk, a Parakeet, an Iranian

I have to come back to domestic assaults again. I know I've been there before, and it might have seemed that there wasn't much more to add, but every day, new cases keep coming up that are so bizarre I am astounded all over again. The lengths that some women will go to ensure their continued abuse boggles my mind.

Consider the husband who smashed his wife across the face with a pool cue. She bailed him out of jail the day before for a DWI, not his first. I guess, in the hopes of making him feel better about how he was screwing up his life, the next day she cooked a nice meal for him and their seven-year-old son. But, being an ass and a drunk, he felt it was not up to his culinary standards and, as punishment for her deficiencies, he got his pool cue and belted her across the face without warning. He's that kind of guy.

She went down, completely senseless, knocked out.

The seven-year-old son dials 911, since he knows how because he's had to do this before when daddy beats mommy.

Daddy, knowing from past experience that when his son dials 911 he ends up in jail, throws junior across the room, trying to keep him from the telephone, and Daddy pockets the phone cord. He's that kind of guy, too.

But the call connected and, with the computerized system installed just the year before, the address showed at police emergency, even though no conversation occurred. The police were dispatched on what is known as a 911 hang-up. They arrived, the seven-year-old avoided Daddy long enough to let them in, and Daddy went to jail — again.

By some miracle, even though the jerk had broken the cue across his wife's face, it didn't cut the skin. I was amazed, because I've seen pool-hall fights where a slash across the top of the head has resulted in over one hundred stitches.

The police brought him to me with two assault charges, and I put him in jail under a $10,000 bond. That should keep him out of circulation, I thought. Who would want to bail him out? Since he has prior assaults and DWI's, such a bond is quite justified, especially since the wife seemed unable to protect herself or their son.

You've probably figured out where I'm going with this story. The next day, honest to God, she was down at the jail trying to get the bondsman who bailed him out on the DWI to get him out again. I wanted to write a warrant for *her* arrest for contributing to child abuse or at least a felonious dumb in public.

Things didn't work the way she had hoped, though. The bondsman was disgusted that she was trying to bail him out again. He revoked his bail on the DWI charge, which added that bail on top of the $10,000, and he told her never to call him again. She spent hours trying to get him out through several different bondsmen, fortunately to no avail. Something very tragic will happen fairly soon in that family. Some people you cannot save from themselves.

The other night, a husband and wife came to the office and asked for me, saying they wanted to get an assault warrant. I was fairly busy at that moment, so instead of asking some preliminary questions to make sure they had the information I would need and whether the police had been involved, I handed them some forms to fill out and told them there would be a wait. They seemed quite agreeable to that. Later I brought them into the office, and they sat beside each other as I put them under oath. Only then did I look over their forms.

"I'm sorry," I apologized, "but I was pretty busy when I explained these forms to you, and I evidently didn't do a very good job. The top of this form is personal information on whoever wants to get a warrant and the second part is the information on the person you want to charge. Now, you have filled these forms out as if you wanted to charge each other with assault."

I expected to see alarm or perhaps humor on their faces at the mistake. What I got were bland looks and both of them nodding their heads affirmatively. Then we all sat there for about ten seconds, eyeing each other. Something new every day.

"Apparently, my explanation of the forms was adequate?"

"Yes," they both answered.

"You want assault warrants against each other?" I'm sure I sounded a little discouraged.

They both nodded, and I had no option but to forge ahead.

I explained to them that they were talking about giving each other criminal records and subjecting each other to the possibility of jail time. They understood that. I also pointed out that the perpetrator and the victim of an assault do not usually sit side by side, almost holding hands. They replied that they liked to consider themselves mature adults, and since it had become clear that they were not going to be able to resolve the problem of who assaulted whom between themselves, they were going to rely on the courts to do that.

There was a certain irrational sense to what they said, but I couldn't get it to go all the way to a rational conclusion. On one side, we had two people sitting demurely together, seeking assault warrants against each other. On my side, we had a magistrate, sitting by himself wondering why he took an oath to do this job.

"I don't suppose the police were involved with this?" I asked, hopefully.

"Why, yes, they were," said the husband, looking startled. "I'm sorry, I forgot to give you the officer's card. He said for you to call him. We came down now because we knew he would be on duty. Our incident occurred yesterday, you see."

I had known the officer for years. He was the most

upbeat cop I had ever known. Always a laugh in his voice, never down. In his profession, a real rarity. I called him.

"Good evening, Officer Brown," I said, as I looked at the couple.

"Mr. Jasper, it's good to hear from you." He was upbeat as always. "Concerning the couple before you now, I thought you'd like to know I've occasionally had to deal with them. Most of the time they get along pretty good. It's only when they stop seeing their respective psychiatrists and stop taking their lithium that they begin to get into problems. You see, they met when they were institutionalized, and they got married after they got better. Oh, and ask them about their witness too."

"I see," I said. But I wasn't sure I did

"I can usually resolve their spats and get them back on their medicine. Maybe I'm losing my touch, or maybe they're losing theirs." He laughed at that and continued, "Whatever, it was a no go this time, so I gave them your name because I knew you would handle it in a most appropriate manner."

"Why thank you, Officer Brown, and I'll surely be talking to you later about this."

"No doubt in my mind, Mr. Jasper, " he chuckled. "Good luck."

I hung up and asked them, "The officer said you have a witness?"

"Yes, Pete, our roommate."

"What does Pete have to say about this?"

"He doesn't want to get involved."

I'd heard that enough times before.

"The officer said it was possible to subpoena witnesses?" the husband asked.

"Yes, that's true. But in situations like this, it's generally not good to do that to someone who doesn't want to take sides. It's a good way to lose a friend — permanently."

"Actually, Pete was the reason for the original disagreement," ventured the wife. "He wouldn't go back after my husband let him out when he shouldn't have."

Seeing that they were getting ready to reargue that point with each other, I cut them off. "Let Pete out? What do you mean let Pete out? Let Pete out of what? I thought he was a roommate."

"He is. He's a roommate and a companion and a friend."

I had a feeling we were close to the essence of the case. "Does this Pete have a last name?"

"No," said the husband, "Just Pete, the parakeet."

Hoo, boy. It took some doing, but I did manage to convince them to go see their counselor before seeking criminal warrants. When they asked when I was working again, I couldn't seem to find my schedule.

On another occasion, at midnight, the police brought before me an Iranian women who had handled matters with her husband in a much more direct manner. It seems that the two were sitting on their bed, planning to have sex, and she was reading the instructions for some type of contraceptive device. I do not know what the device was, as that did not come up in the testimony, and I didn't really want to know anyway. However, the instructions seemed to confuse her so she handed them to her husband to read. I doubt reading several pages of convoluted directions and warnings written by the company's best medical and legal minds was what he really wanted to do at that moment, but she was insistent.

As he struggled with the diagrams and reminders, she got interested in what was on television. Finally, he thought he had it figured out and was all too ready to have a trial run, so to speak. By that time, however, she was interested in the television and was no longer interested in him. He became incensed and made it plain to her what he thought of that and apparently used some highly inappropriate language to her way of thinking. She grabbed a bedside, glass-encased candle and nailed him squarely on the head, which opened a large gash.

The story got a little confusing at that point. He was knocked half senseless and wasn't sure how he ended up cowering in the corner of the room, on the phone with the police, while she repeatedly stabbed at him with a knife.

She was a little vague about it, too, but assured me that she did have him cornered. She certainly didn't seem upset about it at all. Her description to me was delivered in an unemotional, matter-of-fact manner. The officer said that was her demeanor since they arrived at the house.

When the police arrived he was still in the corner on the phone; she continued to brandish the knife. Blood was everywhere, and it wasn't until they got him cleaned up some in the emergency room that it was discovered he had several knife wounds on his hands. He had fended off the knife thrusts with the phone and his hands. She dropped the knife in an offhanded manner when told to do so by the police, and she came along with no protest. This was one icy woman.

After hearing the testimony, I said to her, "This is a very serious charge. Malicious wounding is a felony."

She shrugged and said, "So the police told me."

"Have you been married very long?"

"Seven years."

"Have you had problems?"

"No."

"Can you explain what went wrong tonight?"

She looked confused for a second, as if she didn't know what I was referring to. Then she shrugged again and distractedly answered, "No."

"You realize I'm going to set bail, and you're going to jail?"

"Yes. They also said that could happen." She was very nonchalant about it all.

In situations like hers, some people act similarly, almost with disdain, and then fall apart later. It's not that unusual, but with her I got the feeling I was seeing the real woman. This was not that big a deal with her. It was obvious that she ran the show at home and that she wasn't greatly affected by this contretemps. Must be quite a marriage.

I set bail at $5000, and she didn't bat an eye, asking me if I would take a check.

I said, no, that bail had to be posted in cash only. I thought I hadn't heard right when next she said, "I see. Then my husband will come and pick me up."

I know I must have looked stunned. She wasn't ruffled in the least. It seemed to her a reasonable statement. Did I have a problem with that?

"That's probably not possible," I ventured. "If for

no other reason than he is currently in the emergency room getting stitched up from the cuts you inflicted on him."

She thought on that for a second and then completely confounded me with, "That's okay. I've forgiven him before."

I had no idea what she meant and told the jailors to take her away, which annoyed her very much. She thought I was not very understanding in that I didn't realize how very inconvenient this was for her. Within the hour, she had a bondsman there to bail her out. No question in my mind whether she went home or to the emergency room to check on her husband. I wondered if he had cab fare on him.

"Truth like a bastard comes into the world/
Never without ill-fame to him who gives her birth."
— Thomas Hardy

Chapter 28

Dumb and Dumber

*I*t's usually not a good sign when a phone call begins with, "The police told me to give you a call. They said maybe you'd know the answer . . ."

The woman calling wanted to know how to get an arrest warrant against the locksmith who was giving a new key to her ex-boyfriend every time she had the locks changed. When I suggested using another locksmith, she retorted that all the locksmiths were in cahoots and gave keys to each other, thus ensuring her ex-boyfriend access to her home.

"How long has this been going on with the ex-boyfriend?"

"Twenty-eight years."

"Have you been changing your locks for twenty-eight years?" I asked amazed.

"Yes."

"And your ex-boyfriend has been getting new keys for twenty-eight years?"

"Yes"

I set the phone down and shook my head. It didn't help.

Hoping to clarify things, I asked more directly, "Is he threatening you or what? What do you do when he comes in?"

"Oh, I haven't actually seen him in the apartment, but I know when he's been in there."

"When was the last time you talked to him? Does he admit being in there?"

"I haven't talked to him in eighteen years."

"Eighteen years!" I blurted. "How do you know he's coming into the apartment?"

"The underwear in my drawer changes color."

That stopped the conversation for a few seconds. I must have spent ten minutes on the phone with this woman. No wonder the police gave her my number. I owed them one back. I explained to her, as I've explained to hundreds of others that we handle criminal matters in the magistrate's office. We do not counsel people, or give legal advice, or arbitrate civil disputes or advise on multi-hued underwear. We do spend a lot of time on the phone, however.

I rarely lose my temper. But when I do, it is on the telephone. One day, a young woman called and in a very snotty and demanding manner, which, sad to say is not at all unusual, began with, "The cops said you're to issue a peace bond against my boyfriend."

"Ma'am," I replied, "I doubt if the police told you that. But . . ."

"So, you're not going to help me?" she snapped.

"Ma'am, if you don't let me talk, I can't help you."

Without pause she continued the assault.

"All I've gotten is a bunch of s--t from everybody, and I want something done."

I tried again. "I'm sure we can do something for you, but you've got to listen to me first. Now let . . ."

"Is he going to have to kill me first before you do anything?"

This was one rude woman. Here she was calling for help and arguing with me even before I could finish a sentence. My voice rose a few levels as I said to her, "If you won't listen, I can't help. If you are going to continue to interrupt then I'm going to hang up. Since you did call me for something — I didn't call you — are you going to listen for a few minutes?"

A resentful sounding, "Yes."

I began, but not with much hope, "Magistrates rarely issue peace bonds on a pretrial basis. However, if your situation is such that you feel the need for one, the odds are that he probably has committed a criminal act that we can write an arrest warrant for and put him in jail. While he is in jail, you can go to a judge and ask for what is called a 'preliminary protective' order. That is served on him in jail. If he bonds out, it forbids him to have any contact with you, and if you are living together it forbids him to return home. An emergency hearing is set within five days. You and he go before a judge, and the judge hears both sides, deciding whether to continue the order or change it or end it. If, at any time, he has any contact with you, the judge will issue a bench warrant for his arrest for violating the order, and he will be held without bond. Do you understand so far?"

Another resentful "Yes."

"Now, if he has assaulted you or threatened you, you can come down now to the magistrate's office, and I'll listen to you under oath. If I feel he has committed a crime, I'll write a warrant and have him locked up. The rest, about your going to see a judge, is up to you after that. It's not what you are calling a 'peace bond,' but it gets him arrested and in jail, and it gives you time to see a judge about a protective order, which is better than a peace bond. Do you understand what you need to do?"

To my immense dissatisfaction, she replied, "So you're not going to do anything for me, and he can just do anything he damn well wants, is that it?"

For a brief moment I was too amazed to even respond. But then the adrenalin kicked in. "I don't know where you were the last five minutes," I yelled, "but you obviously weren't listening to me! I can't help you. I can't do anything for you. All the judges are on vacation and the jail's full. If you get killed, call next week and ask for an appointment!"

I slammed the phone down hard enough to knock it off the desk. My outburst didn't make a bit of sense, but she didn't call back, either.

On the subject of denseness, I must relate some occurrences to illustrate that the criminals, dupes, and contributory victims do not have a complete corner on that market. Various officers have, through the years, shown some remarkably unimaginative thinking. A particular female sergeant, recently promoted, was having a difficult time in her new job. She'd had a hard time being even an adequate patrol officer, but the chief wanted to promote females. She had a college degree and always tested well, but when it came to common sense, she knew nothing. Not helpful, either, was her personality — arrogant condescension, which she used to cover her lack of confidence. She didn't have a clue as to how to be a sergeant. She responded by trying to be everywhere and do everything. Which was why she was involved in a foot pursuit, one night, instead of supervising.

She spotted two guys, walking down the street, she knew were wanted. Trying to be superwoman, she jumped from her cruiser, shouted, "Freeze," and attempted to arrest both by herself. She had taken on a couple of wise, tough, street-smart ex-cons, who were not going to faint from fright. She managed to grab one and wrestle him to the ground as your average superwoman would. While trying to handcuff him and rolling in the dirt, she screamed at the other one again, not to move. Fortunately, instead of bashing her head in, which would not have been difficult since she didn't have the first guy under control at all, he took off like an Olympic sprinter. Superwoman status did not impress him any more than loyalty to his friend.

She did manage to get a cuff on the guy on the ground. But she was enraged that the other guy had dared to ignore her command. She wanted him too. She had to do something with the first guy though. She snapped the other end of the cuff around a convenient street sign and was off like a shot, at least in her mind. The chase was in vain; he was long gone. She hated not to be able to make a double arrest and kept searching, but the fleeing felon had flown. At least she got one and called for the paddy wagon to meet her at Elm Street and 4th Avenue, where he was handcuffed.

The wagon got there before she did, and when she walked up to the waiting, burly cop, he said, "Where's the bad guy, Sarge?"

"I thought you had him in the wagon already."

"Wasn't nobody here when I drove up."

"I cuffed him to the street sign." There was concern and doubt in her voice.

She immediately ran to where the street sign had been half an hour before and found only a hole in the ground.

"S--t!" said Sergeant Superwoman.

The wagon driver couldn't resist, "I guess we better start looking for a man handcuffed to a street sign and a concrete footing. Shouldn't be too hard to spot, huh Sarge. And besides, he'll probably be right at Elm Street and 4th Avenue when we find him."

A veteran detective gave me testimony one day about an attempt to obtain a prescription by fraud. He had arrested a woman who showed up at a drug store with a forged prescription for fifty Percocet tablets, a very strong and addictive pain reliever. It was a poorly done forgery, and the pharmacist called the police immediately while stalling the woman. She was arrested, interrogated by the detective, and brought to jail. The detective's testimony was complete and detailed and sufficient for me to issue a warrant for prescription fraud, which I told him I would do.

He then added, "I'd also like to get a warrant for conspiracy to obtain drugs."

That surprised me greatly, since nobody else had been mentioned in the testimony. "Did I miss something here?" I asked. "With whom did she conspire?"

He looked at me rather sternly and said, "The code says it can be charged."

I told him I was unaware of that, but we could look it up right there and see. It read, "If any person conspires with another to obtain a prescription drug by fraud or deceit he shall be guilty of a class six felony." I looked at the detective and asked again, "Who is the other person?"

To which he replied doggedly, "Someone."

I was stumped. "Who is *someone*?"

"I don't know."

"You don't mean the accused that I've already written a warrant against?"

"No."

"It takes two people for a conspiracy."

"Well," he said, "she's any person."

"Who's any person?"

"She is. It's in the code"

This was beginning to sound like the Abbott and Costello bit of "Who's on first?" I explained, "You can't conspire with yourself, if that's what you're suggesting. You have to have 'another,' just like the code says."

"But, she's *any* person," he tried again.

"I agree she's *any* person, I suppose, but just being *any* person doesn't make you guilty of conspiracy." I was having a hard time trying to explain a concept in the face of an argument based on a precept that the detective had in his mind. I didn't have a clue what he meant — I think.

"Well, sir," he pouted, "I think it's a legitimate

charge, but if you don't want to write it, I won't push
for it"

I wondered what he thought he had been doing
for the last ten minutes. To this day, the detective
still seems to think he had a conspiracy of one; a
classic case of not wanting to be confused by the
facts.

The sheriff's department has its moments, too.
Working a midnight shift full of drunks one weekend, I sent a list over to the booking desk, at about
4:00 a.m., of about twenty-five drunks who I wanted
brought over for release. It was clearly titled at the
top — 5:00 a.m. releases. A few minutes later the
booking deputy called on the phone and asked, "What
time do you want the five a.m. releases?"

I hesitated, and when he said nothing more, I suggested, "Oh, say five a.m.?"

Oblivious to it all, he replied crisply, "You got it,
sir."

Chapter 29

"3" Is for Allute

*W*e, the magistrates, may now lay down our quill pens and set aside our ink wells; we are computerized. The computers have arrived and are installed. Also today, coincidentally, the sewer system backed up and our toilet overflowed for about an hour. Since there is about six inches of evil-smelling sewage sloshing around our office, *ain't nobody* going near all those pretty new computers. Not a very auspicious beginning for our own personal computer age.

One of our madam magistrates came flying out of the bathroom sounding the alarm. She had flushed, and instead of going down, everything came up! Immediately behind her came the deluge.

With no concern whatsoever for anybody else's welfare, I was out the door and heading for high ground. Not that anyone else stayed behind to try and stem the tide. I wasn't first out the door by much as the seething mess gurgled, hissed, and routed the office of all opposition. We, the opposition, did eventually creep back down the stairs for a peek. I clearly remember dark water, toilet paper, and bobbing things — yuk.

"Ladies and gentlemen," I declared, "I will be at my home until the present crisis is resolved. I believe the facilities maintenance people can cope quite well without my assistance."

The disagreeable flood was eventually cleaned up with a lot of hard work from several of the jail trustees. There was a lot of wrangling with facilities maintenance about getting the carpet replaced. They seemed to be under the very mistaken impression that with some vigorous wet-vacuuming and liberal dispensing of disinfectant, the office could be opened for business as usual. When your office is in the basement of the jail, you get no respect from anyone.

I pointed out to the maintenance people that there was encrusted toilet paper clinging to the walls at the high-water mark, and it would be a very cold day in hell before we stayed in there under those conditions. They eventually, grudgingly, acceded and did strip the lower walls and replace the fouled carpet. It was pretty obvious that they really didn't think we were worth all that expense and effort.

We won, not because we were magistrates, but because we outnumbered the maintenance people, threatened to start beating up people and having sit-ins, sixties style, in the courthouse. That meant the possibility of the newspapers becoming interested, and that always scares the hell out of the courthouse powers that be. Since those powers always considered magistrates loose cannons anyway, our wishes were met; if only to get us back in the basement and once again out of sight. So, after several days in temporary quarters, we returned to our scrubbed and newly carpeted cesspool to begin life anew as computerized, sanitized officers of the court.

Our computers are a mixed blessing. They ask a lot of dumb questions which make me wonder about the programmers in Richmond. For "sex of the accused," one can choose "male," "female" or "other." Other? There are fourteen different choices for race, including "R" for black Hispanic, "Q" for white Hispanic, and "Z" for Allute. The nationwide computer system that all this is entered into accepts only W — white, B — black, and O — oriental. Q, Z, and R, it does not know. Such wonderful interagency integration is not encouraging.

Also exceedingly irritating is that if one wishes to change the suggested wording of a warrant, which is often, since criminals don't always break the law in precisely the manner dictated by the wording from Richmond, it must be laboriously deleted, letter by letter, before proceeding. Richmond explains such quirks in their statewide system by asserting that they have certain "priorities." That's bureaucratic hyperbole, we've discovered, for "Screw you. It's easier for us to do it our way."

On the other hand, once the entries are made, things go quickly, especially if the accused is charged with more than one offense. As with all new things, we're slowly getting to know each other; however, it is a bit tiresome for we humans to have to change our methods every time there is a conflict on technique with the computer. The computer loses no arguments and tolerates no obstreperousness on the part of mere mortals. But if one acts properly (the magistrates, I mean), the benefits of not having to write out in laborious longhand all the warrants, releases, etc., become quickly apparent.

While on the subject of technology, the other day I was handed a teletype from another state, requesting that we issue a fugitive warrant for a John Refnagle, wanted by them and presently in our jail.

There was a problem. There was no John Refnagle in our jail. A great deal of rechecking and verifying occurred. Not only was he not in jail, he had never been in our jail. Even further searching showed no John Refnagle anywhere in the Commonwealth of Virginia in anybody's jail. We had arrived at a dead end. Certainly not the first dead-end computer search I had ever been involved in, nor would it be the last. But this time, as I sat pondering the teletype, I had a rare brainstorm. I checked for John Nagle, and his name appeared as "in residence," a guest of the county.

The failure of a clerk to hit the space bar on his teletype had changed Reference Nagle

REF-NAGLE, JOHN

to REFNAGLE, JOHN. Such are the problems we've created with our exacting technologies for our not-so-exacting minds.

Those same minds have created laws with some amazing contradictions. Concerning teletypes, in Virginia there is a beauty. The law says that if an officer in one county has someone in custody and receives a teletype from another county that they have an arrest warrant for that person, then that individual can be arrested. There is a problem, though, that I had noted a few years earlier and asked Uncle Billy about. I pointed out to him that, according to that law, a teletype from your own county could not be used to arrest someone within that same county, only the actual warrant could be used to make an arrest.

Billy never did like any of my questions. I don't think he really disliked *me*, but then I was never sure about that because Billy kept his emotions and feelings very closely guarded. He never made trouble for me. He tolerated me, that's about the best way I could describe our relationship. I never took it personally because it seemed as if that was Billy's relationship with the rest of the world too. I did ask a lot of questions, though, and at times I'm sure I was very wearing for him.

I pointed out to him that when an arrest warrant is written locally for someone living in another county, the warrant is mailed by the police to that county. If the police there can't find him, it is eventually mailed back. I said to Billy that I could see a problem if the warrant was in the mail when our police stumbled across the bad guy. The code was poorly written, which is more the norm than the exception. Most state legislatures are liberally sprinkled with lawyers and vaguely written laws mean fully employed lawyers.

Uncle Billy, true to form, said maybe so but it would be so rare it would probably never happen. That was vintage Uncle Billy. If it's not a problem today, don't bother me.

Of course, it did happen. But in a way Billy was right, because when it did, Billy had long since retired, and it wasn't his problem. The county police, acting on a tip, arrested a guy wanted for robbery. They had been looking for him. The warrant was in the mail to the Norfolk Police. His only known address was that of his mother in Norfolk. The police quite properly brought him before a magistrate with a teletype from their own police department stating they had a warrant for him that was in the mail. What else could the police do? Ask this dirtball to please hang around the neighborhood for a few days until the warrant was retrieved and then turn himself in? The magistrate committed him to jail.

At arraignment the next morning, the chief judge of the general district court said just that and refused to hold an arraignment. The fact that a robbery suspect with an extensive record was off the street impressed him not at all. All too often, reason and common sense suffer ignominious defeat when toe to toe with the legal system.

Wiser heads hustled the bad guy out of the court room before said judge could do something stupid like order him released, which was a very real possibility. Eventually, another judge, known to possess a modicum of common sense, was approached, and using reason and practical judgment he confirmed the bond set by the magistrate, ensuring the robber stayed in jail.

Finally, in the technological bag of tricks there is the ubiquitous answering machine. Despised by telemarketers, it has become indispensable to many. There was an electrical contracting company that had a very good employee whom they prized highly. Their man had always liked his booze, but until the last two years it wasn't a problem. However, it was now becoming a problem, so the contractor told him he had to stop drinking or they would, reluctantly, have to fire him. The employee liked his job, was good at it and was well paid. He stopped drinking. But his wife, who also had a drinking problem but did not have a job, kept on boozing. Her husband, newly sober, realized after a few weeks of sobriety that he was married to a drunk and discovered he didn't like drunks. He gave her an ultimatum: stop drinking or he was leaving.

Mulling over this most unpleasant development, she concluded that her problems were the fault of her husband's employer. If that bastard had just left her husband alone, he'd still be sharing drinks with her. The fact that he would also be unemployed was lost in her alcoholic haze. Alcoholics are not real strong in the logic department. She began calling the contractor several times a day, always drunk and always abusive. He was a remarkably forgiving man and put up with it for several days until he finally told her he was no longer going to listen to her drunken, abusive ramblings.

Since he wouldn't talk to her anymore, she decided one evening to call his office phone and for two full hours, until the tape ran out, repeated the word "f--k" as many times as she could on his answering machine. She recited it, chanted it, rhymed it, screamed it. She even sang it to the melody of "The Star Spangled Banner." That in itself was a tour de force.

It was finally enough to push the contractor over the edge and he ended up at the magistrate's office. I wrote a warrant for using abusive language on the telephone. I didn't have to wonder what she would say when the police came to arrest her.

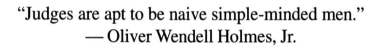
"Judges are apt to be naive simple-minded men."
— Oliver Wendell Holmes, Jr.

Chapter 30

Is There a Doctor In the Jail?

I have yet to write an arrest warrant for a priest. In light of recent news stories, it appears only a matter of time before Father P. D. O'Phile is before me. Who can you trust anymore?

We are probably more trusting of our doctors than any other people with whom we come in contact. We often quite literally put our lives in their hands. They are human, though, and even their best efforts are, at times, in vain. We used to be more forgiving when one gave one's best. With all the underemployed lawyers out there now, it's no wonder that many doctors feel more like targets than healers. But the profession still commands a respect far above any other, so when a doctor acts unprofessionally, it's very disturbing. When one acts like a raging maniac, it's terrifying.

She was a physician and a surgeon, and so drunk

that traffic was backed up behind her on the interstate for a mile because of her weaving from one
side of the highway to the other. Nobody wanted to
chance trying to get by.

A state trooper eventually worked his way to the
front of the backup and felt his stomach drop when he
saw three children in the car. She ignored his lights,
siren, and loudspeaker, refusing to stop. He had to get
her stopped quickly before a terrible tragedy occurred.
He took a deep breath, said a small prayer, and to his
great credit managed to box her in by himself and get
her stopped with only very minor damage and no injuries.

Troopers in Virginia make little money, have a
lousy retirement plan, deal every day with mangled
bodies in horrific wrecks and routinely risk their lives
for other people. They are unfailingly polite and highly
professional.

She fought him from the very beginning. He managed to get her out of the car while she cursed him
with some of the foulest language imaginable and
kicked at him repeatedly. As her children looked on,
he had to subdue her and handcuff her. Her language
and threats never slowed down as she continued trying to kick the trooper in the groin.

She refused to give the name of someone who could
come for her children, since she was going to jail. She
screamed at the trooper to f--k off. It was the oldest
boy, ten and scared to death, who gave the trooper a
neighbor's name and phone number, while his drunken
mother raved and cursed. Throughout the whole or-
deal, even when she was finally brought to me, she
threatened the trooper that she would get him fired

and make him pay dearly for this. He was used to hearing that. But then the threats took an extremely ugly turn. She repeated several times that she hoped she would be on duty in the emergency room some night and he would come in injured and she could throw his ass out on the street. It was a shocking thing to hear.

As I tried to listen to the trooper's testimony, she screamed obscenities at him and me and began promising to butcher any state trooper she would be lucky enough to get on her operating table. Her screaming hatred of the trooper unnerved me. She promised to hurt him any way she could, over and over and over. She made it clear that when she got out she would long for the day she could cripple him and mangle him.

The trooper never lost his cool and acted like a gentleman. I don't know how, but he maintained his composure throughout. When the deputies searched her purse, it was found to be loaded with several different pain killers. Drugs, alcohol, psychotic behavior — and she was operating on people. It's a chilling thought.

She was charged with DWI and prescription fraud. She hired lawyers and expert witnesses and won acquittals from a very new judge who, quite simply, got intimidated and overwhelmed by the high-priced firepower brought to bear. The medical board declined to revoke her license and seemed satisfied with a mild letter of reprimand for unprofessional behavior. She is still operating on people today. Not a very proud day for judges or doctors, but a very bad day for patients.

Two other cases involving doctors, while not nearly as vicious, were just as worrisome as both involved sexual assaults on patients in the examining room. To be sexually assaulted when seeking help, comfort and relief from pain is particularly odious. To take advantage of such a trust is despicable. The cases were unrelated and I heard them months apart, but both women had the same reluctance to proceed on to prosecution.

They both felt deep disappointment and distress, but a lack of hostility towards the respective doctors. They expressed to me that they felt a duty to proceed only to protect other possible future victims. Punishment for what was done to them was not their primary interest. I would have expected outrage and a desire to tear the doctor limb from limb. If it had been anybody but a doctor, I suspect they would have felt similarly. They both had many conflicting emotions to contend with, but both women testified and both doctors were convicted.

The first, an orthopedic surgeon, had been charged with attempted rape and eventually agreed to a lesser charge of sexual molestation and court-ordered psychiatric counselling. His license to practice was suspended by the state medical board, which reserved the right to revoke it permanently at the end of his one-year probation ordered by the court. I assume it was not revoked outright because the doctor had an unblemished history.

The second, a gynecologist, was charged with sodomy and convicted. His record was not unblemished as there had been patient complaints before. He served time in prison and had his license revoked permanently.

I admired the women because it took great courage to do what they did, and their reason for doing so was the purest — to protect others from what they had gone through. Their determination to do what they felt was right, knowing they were facing some very hostile cross examination in court and the possibility of being sued, inspired me. I hope they are doing well today.

C.I.A. employees don't have the standing in the community enjoyed by doctors, but they are professional people and on occasion get arrested for DWI. I know I have one when, during the bond hearing, I ask, "Where do you work?" Only the unemployed and C.I.A. employees have a problem with that question. The unemployed know that joblessness is not looked upon with favor by the court. The spooks seem to feel there is a spy behind every magistrate.

I am somewhat bemused with the C.I.A. There are many excellent people in the organization and some of the most intelligent, hardest-working people I have ever met were C.I.A. employees. Still, in light of recent spy scandals and the apparent failure of the C.I.A. to ever figure out what was going on inside the Soviet Union, which was pretty much their original *raison d'etre*, one has to wonder if there was not an occasional misdirection of effort in Langley. Their employees under arrest are exquisitely polite and acutely embarrassed.

"Mr. Smith, you have a mandatory court appearance for this charge. I need to assure myself that you will be there, so I have to ask you some personal questions to determine whether you can be released or not."

"Certainly."

"Have you ever been arrested before?'

"No, sir."

"Are you married or single?'

"Married, sir."

"Are you renting or buying your home?"

"Buying, sir."

"And where do you work, Mr. Smith?'

"I'm very sorry, sir, but I'm not at liberty to divulge that information, sir."

With that answer everybody within earshot, including the almost comatose drunk on the bench behind Mr. Smith, knows he works for the C.I.A.. I persist, "Mr. Smith, the more I know about you, the better your chances of being released. How come you didn't just tell me you work for the state department like everybody else in your line of work?"

"I'm sorry, sir, I can't talk about my job."

"But Mr. Smith, the cold war's over — we won. And, besides, I won't tell anybody anyway."

A polite, wish-I-could-help smile from Mr. Smith. I'm sure he considers me a bit too flip on a very serious matter down at the Agency. I always persist, though.

"Heard any good Aldrich Ames jokes lately?"

Mr. Smith looks understandably pained at that low blow.

"Would you at least agree to the statement that you are employed by the U.S. Government, Mr. Smith?"

"I'm very sorry, sir, I just can't discuss it."

"How about, are you a U.S. citizen?"

"I am that, sir."

"Good enough."

I always end up releasing the Mr. Smiths of the C.I.A. after the alcohol is out. It wouldn't be right to not let someone go whose loyalty to his oath is so strong that he will go to jail rather than violate it. But just once it would be wonderful for someone to say, "Yes I do work for the C.I.A., and if you look into my tie tac I'll take your picture."

On the subject of oddball arrests, I hold the record for committing the oldest man to jail. He was eighty years old and just as much a crook now as he was in 1929 when he was first arrested. For sixty-five years, the only time this man was not stealing, cheating or robbing was when he was in prison. A printout of his complete record would probably take hours. He was the definition of incorrigible and seemed determined to pass his experience on, since when he was arrested this last time he had a fifteen-year-old boy with him.

The old man was slowly driving a car along the front of several stores in a shopping strip while the boy ducked into stores and stole whatever came to hand easily. They were working so quickly that he never had to stop the car as they moved down the strip. The only time the car did stop was when they came to a liquor store and gramps ambled into the store and out again with a couple bottles of booze. Fortunately, there just happened to be two undercover cops nearby, watching the whole escapade in amazement.

They brought the old man to me and took the kid to juvenile holding. The officer said, and I thought correctly, "He may be old, but he's also a bastard and a reprobate. And now he's using kids because he's too crotchety to do the stealing himself. Except for liquor stores, of course."

The old boy wasn't concerned in the least. After all, Calvin Coolidge was president and talking pictures were a brand-new innovation when he was first arrested. He didn't have much to say, just a general, for-the-record declaration of his complete innocence and that he "didn't know nothin' about no boy shoplifting." It was just some kid he was giving a ride to. A real piece of work he was. Eighty or not, especially since his health was good, he was going to jail, charged with various thefts and contributing to the delinquency of a minor. I asked him if he had ever heard of Charles Dickens or a dude named Fagin.

He squinted at me, shrugged his shoulders, and said slyly, "I might know 'em. If yer lookin' for 'em, I might be able to help if you go easy on my bond." The old boy was a pro all right, looking to work every angle possible all the time, even if he didn't know what the hell I was talking about.

"No, you can't help there," I said. "Charlie's gone now, but you didn't miss him by too many years. If you'd ever met Fagin, you two would have hit it off immediately, I'm sure."

I nodded to the deputy and in my best voice called, "Take him down constable, take him down to the cells in the name of the Queen."

Chapter 31

Pet-o-phile Grannies

The mail did not get delivered in more ways than one when a postman in uniform was arrested in the public restroom of a department store for soliciting a homosexual act. A security guard waiting alertly in one of the stalls, because of previous complaints from shoppers about such unwanted intrusions, had taken a photograph of a fully erect penis pushed under the partition. Yes, I know, it seemed pretty weird to me, too — not only the postman but the guard. I wondered what the guard tells his children he does for a living.

The postman had put up a hell of a fight when he realized he was going to be arrested and kept from completing his appointed rounds. He had been brought in, though, and as I sat looking at the photo of the evidence, which I had to admit was considerable, one of the female magistrates looking over my shoulder murmured, "Wuff, that doesn't look like *my* mailman at all."

I looked at her. She smiled at me, raised her eyebrows, and strolled away.

"Who's sexually harassing whom around her?" I asked no one in particular.

One day a seventy-year-old woman ran afoul of the bare-knuckles environment in the magistrate's office. An animal control warden (once known as a dog catcher) came to me for an assault warrant against the woman. I was, initially, somewhat skeptical since the warden was about thirty years old, six feet tall, and in robust good health.

It was not busy when the warden came in, so I had two other magistrates listening with interest as I heard his testimony. The woman was known to the wardens. She had been collecting stray cats and dogs for the last two years and keeping them in her house. No problem with that. Her intentions were initially laudable. However, the number had grown to over one hundred, and the neighbors had begun to complain because her backyard had become so foul with cat and dog feces that there was not one square millimeter not covered with the stuff. The stench was indescribable.

My brother and his wife have six cats, and I fed them and cleaned their litter boxes (the cats') for a few days once when they (my brother and his wife) were out of town. That chore just about gagged me every day, so I could not imagine the smell of a whole yard full of the stuff.

So many neighbors complained that the wardens went to the house to talk to the old lady. She opened the door a crack and told them all to go to hell and get off her property. But through the crack they had seen enough. Excrement was everywhere: stuck on the walls, encrusted in the rug, plastered on some sick-looking, mangy animals. Such situations are not as rare as one would think. The wardens had handled such cases before and knew what to do. They obtained a search warrant from a magistrate for entry into the house and confiscation of all maltreated animals. I have issued such warrants, and it frequently involves older single women, who are called by some, "pet-o-phile grannies."

This particular granny, though, was a real pain. She refused them entry when they showed up with the search warrant, and the wardens finally had to break her door to gain access. I must point out that they don't break doors down with a battering ram like it was a drug raid. Some gentle prying with a small bar is all that's needed for the door to pop open. Most of these grannies are cantankerous, but none has yet responded with an Uzi. I'm sure there will be a first.

They found what they have come to expect: dead and dying cats and dogs, excrement, and filth throughout the house, flea, roach, and mice infestation, and a smell that required them to wear gas masks. A bathtub half full of some black witches' brew that allegedly had once been water, but now had a few inches of crust on the top, was a little rougher than usual. How granny stood the stink amazed everyone. But then she smelled like everything else in the house, too, and was she outraged.

She called the wardens every name she could think of and repeatedly tried to hit anyone within range with her cane. Whenever she got the chance, she would sneak up behind a warden and slug him with it. She was not a frail woman at all, and the wardens concluded that she carried a cane mainly for offensive purposes. She packed a pretty mean wallop. Finally, they took her cane from her, and a police officer made her stay seated on the couch. She continued vilifying them nonstop during the several hours they were there removing animals.

Many of the animals taken to the shelter had to be put to sleep because they were in such bad shape. Granny was not one to be intimidated and attempted several times in the following weeks to visit what she considered "prisoners" at the animal shelter. Whenever she arrived, it was in a wheelchair, due to injuries she said she had suffered at the hands of the Gestapo troopers who had stormed her house. She was firmly denied admission.

The warden requesting the assault warrant had been hit a few times by granny on the day of the search, but he didn't want a warrant for that, as he figured that was part of the job and she was seventy years old. He was more forgiving than I would have been. She had been forbidden to visit the animals in the shelter, since they had been legally taken from her pending a hearing. On this particular day, in spite of being denied access on all previous days, she was not to be deterred, and in her wheelchair rolled through the front desk, cane swinging with determination. In her mind, it was an assault on the bastion of the storm troopers. She could play tough, too.

The warden was in the back when he heard the commotion and on the way to the front encountered granny in the hall, pedal to the metal, fire in her eyes. She rammed him at full speed, putting a nasty gash in his leg, and with all her strength swung her cane with both hands at his knee, connecting solidly. As the warden said while showing me a very swollen knee, "This old lady has slugged me, gashed me, cussed me, and damn near crippled me with her cane. Enough is enough, seventy years old or not."

The other magistrates applauded. Idle magistrates can act strangely. I wrote a warrant for assault.

In due course, they brought the old lady before me in her wheelchair. She was playing it for all she was worth, moaning and sobbing, but occasionally sneaking a peek to see how she was doing. My colleagues were quite free with their advice, stage whispering such things as, "Does AARP membership get you a free lawyer?" and, "Don't forget the senior citizen discount when you set bond." What did they care? Their names weren't on anything.

But the more I thought about it, and the more I watched her award-winning histrionics, the more I agreed enough was enough. She horribly mistreated several animals and acted in despicable ways toward the authorities who were trying only to lessen the misery of those animals that were unable to protect themselves. She was arrogant, condescending, and she reeked.

"One thousand dollar bond. Commit her to jail," I heard myself say. She gasped, the warden gaped. Even the jailors were momentarily bug-eyed. She began to squawk, but they rolled her away. My magistrate colleagues were content.

"Good, you didn't let her Oscar performance throw you off."

"Put her on bread and water. It's more than she gave the kitties and puppies," added another.

I felt pretty good about putting her in the slammer. Maybe too good. She was, after all, seventy years old. Was I doing something wrong here? Then I remembered the ghastly pictures of the sick and dying animals.

Every so often something does occur that makes me wonder if it is time for a career change. An officer came in not too long ago, looking a little pale. So much so that I asked him about it.

"Oh, I've been in the emergency room for a couple hours. I worked a bad DWI wreck. Guy was doing eighty on a back road, lost it, went airborne, got sideways, and wrapped himself around a tree. His buddy, passed out drunk in the back seat, got killed instantly. The driver drove his legs through the floor panel. Smashed his feet and peeled his skin and muscles up to almost his knees. When I got there he's still screaming. Sure am glad I hadn't had anything to eat yet — pretty grisly looking."

I agreed it sounded pretty gross.

"Yeh, and I've been in the emergency room for two hours while they're trying to figure if they can save his legs. Well, I need a DWI warrant for the moment. I'll be back later looking for a manslaughter warrant."

I said, "How about I give you a summons instead of a warrant. That way you don't have to arrest him and get stuck with a police guard until he's released from the hospital. It sounds like that could be a while.

I don't think he's going to run away."

The officer started laughing, and it took me a second to realize what I'd said. I thought it was somewhat funny, too. Here's a case where a guy killed his friend and crippled himself for life, and the cop and I were laughing. And then the cop added that he helped put a catheter in the guy at the crash scene, and while he was doing it, the guy kept yelling about how much it hurt. But the cop thought, fine, you stupid bastard, I hope it hurts. You just killed your buddy, and he can't feel anything, good or bad — ever again.

The officer got his summons and headed back to the hospital, and I sat there feeling quite normal; as if we had been discussing a minor fender bender. Only hours later did I begin to think the conversation was a little weird, but even in retrospect I don't think it was very weird. Even as I'm writing this I don't think it was that weird. I think that maybe the cop and the catheter was a little odd. However, I'm sure the cop doesn't think it was that much out of line.

Laughter is a defense, and it works. It's human, normal, and necessary. But every such tragedy, every sad case, takes a little piece out of you, torn off into the void. You know it, and you laugh. Human nature seems to be perverse that way, "Go ahead, take a piece of me. I laugh at you for doing so. I have many pieces. It does not bother me." Only, many pieces later I will cry.

"He who permits himself to tell a lie once, finds it much easier to do it a second and third time, till at length it becomes habitual."
— Thomas Jefferson

Chapter 32

The Finger

We're not being very polite to each other these days. A young lady came to me and said, "I called the police, and they said maybe you could issue a warrant for something called curse and abuse?"

I told her that, yes, there was such a charge but that we don't do it very often. Times are such that even at the better restaurants the language you hear in everyday conversation at the table next to you is filled with four-letter expletives. Even on prime-time television, there seem to be very, very few remaining constraints on bad taste and foul language. I asked her to briefly tell me what the situation was.

She said, "I can tell you real briefly. Some foreigner cab driver took me from the airport to my home. He didn't know any of the streets and got lost three times. I thought I was going to have to drive because he couldn't understand directions, either. In spite of that and the fact that he didn't help me with my luggage and he smelled like a goat, I gave him a tip anyway. God knows why. He thought he deserved more and started yelling at me. I'd had it with him, and I told him so. Then he screamed even louder at me, calling me a 'f--king c--t' and said that in his country he would have had my tongue cut out. He's the one that called me a 'f--king c--t.' How about his tongue? What a dirtball camel jockey."

I thought a warrant appropriate in this case. She thought deportation would be nice too. But I told her not to hold out too much hope for that. I.N.S. doesn't seem to get very interested until someone has a few murders behind them or a few tons of heroin for sale. As a matter of fact, in twelve years I've known the I.N.S. to show up at the jail a grand total of one time and it wasn't for a cabbie who had insulted his fare.

I suppose then, I shouldn't have been upset the day a young punk came to the window and asked in a belligerent voice, "Hey man, where do I go piss in the bottle?" I debated in my mind several equally offensive answers before deciding, why bother? I just simply directed him to the drug-screening office. The word "piss" is used quite often on television now and seems to be as acceptable as damn. It doesn't seem right, somehow.

Rudeness can also be extremely dangerous, especially in traffic. Many people seem to drive with one hand on the wheel while giving the finger to any and all other drivers who dare impede their progress. When two such rudenesses meet, there can be fist fights, car bashing, and gunfire.

In one case I handled, both drivers got out with "The Club." One ended up in the hospital with a broken jaw and the loss of an eye.

Giving the finger seems to have evolved into what many feel is a constitutional right. I have heard both those assaulted and those accused say in wonderment, "I don't know what he was so pissed about. All I did was give him the finger."

When I point out that it is an extremely offensive and inciting gesture, I invariably get an argument that some people deserve getting the finger. It's as if it was their civic duty to deliver the message.

I was explaining bond to a man, who had been arrested for breaking up his landlady's furniture. He tried to tell me he was an alcoholic and, by implication, he should not be charged because he was not responsible for his actions — another bleating that I have grown very weary of hearing. I told him I didn't want to hear that line of phony psychobabble. What was his response? The finger! The arresting cop's eyes about popped out when he saw it.

For some reason, it didn't upset me. I found it more disheartening than anything else. I just thought, The Finger, a sign of our times. I set a digitally induced bond of $5,000.

It bothers me when I am waiting in line at the 7-Eleven to see how rude people are to the poor, overworked, minimum-waged clerks. Rarely do they even get a "Please" or ~thank you." Most people are worse than condescending, they're contemptuous. One's life must be very pathetic if sneering at the 7-Eleven clerk is the highlight of the day.

When people are being rude to me, I can't tell if it's because of the office I hold and they mean to act rudely, or if they don't have a clue as to what polite conduct is and wouldn't recognize it if they fell over it. Either way, I'm not very encouraged. People come to the window and rap on it vigorously for attention even when they can see quite clearly that I am extremely busy at that moment.

I always point out to them how rude that is. Invariably they tell me how important their time is and that they are late for a very important meeting with other very important people. When I inform them that their rudeness has earned them a ten-minute penalty in the box for snottiness, they don't understand what I'm talking about until I disappear and attend to other matters for ten minutes.

No one has yet to be contrite for their bad manners. Quite the opposite, they tend to wrap themselves with self-righteous indignation under such circumstances. Rude people make many demands. I respond to none of them. And since society seems to reward those who are obnoxious and demanding, I go out of my way to be as helpful as I possibly can be to those who act civilly and decently.

Phone manners also seem to be nonexistent. Most people have at least heard of manners for face-to-face encounters, even if they don't often use them. But the anonymity of the telephone seems to encourage rudeness. People call seeking help and burp in my ear while eating lunch or ask the dog if it wants to go outside for a dump. They turn the television up so as not to miss a word of Jerry or Jenny and then yell in the phone. They have a simultaneous talk with the kids about wiping their feet, or don't want to get off the speakerphone when I tell them they're unintelligible. I have asked people to please take the gum out of their mouths because I can't understand what they are saying, and in response I have been cursed at and had the phone slammed down in my ear.

One of my pet peeves is people who call for directions to the magistrate's office and, when I start, they say, "Wait, I need to go find a pen and paper." Then they expect you to ignore everything else you may have been doing while they rummage all over the house for a lousy piece of paper. When they eventually do get back to the phone, the pen doesn't work, and they're off again.

I know without a doubt it would enrage them if they were the ones having to wait, so why do they do it to me? Those who are particularly unpleasant when seeking directions, I give our address, tell them to go to the 7-Eleven nearest their home and buy a street map, look up the address, and proceed accordingly. I am careful to do it very politely, though. That's important.

Even the phone companies are encouraging rudeness and making a profit on it. I don't know how many times someone called and asked to speak to a magistrate and, as soon as they got one — namely me —tried to put me on hold to answer their call waiting. They don't even ask. They say, "I've got to answer my call waiting. I'll be back." Then, click.

I hang up one hundred times out of one hundred. I'm far from the most important person in the world, but please don't insult me to my face while you see if somebody more important is calling.

Call Waiting is also a sign of our times, along with The Finger.

". . . some people are a little bit guilty,
while other people are guilty as hell."
— Donald R. Cressey

Chapter 33

A Situation

Some cases are just plain tough to handle. Nothing satisfying about the resolution and a general bad feeling about the whole thing that can last for days or weeks. They make me wince even today.

An officer came to me one day and said, "I sure am glad you're the magistrate and not me 'cause I've got a situation for you that's really bad."

The police use a lot of terms to describe predicaments they're not sure about. The terms they use often unconsciously indicate the seriousness involved. It's far from one hundred percent, but it's right often enough. They don't realize that when they say a "can of worms" as in "I got a can of worms here," it's usually not all that bad, but probably pretty confusing. With some concentrated listening and then some coaxing from the magistrate, the officer generally works it out satisfactorily. The police don't have anybody under arrest when they have a can of worms.

When the officer shows up with "a real mess," he usually has several people under arrest and he's not sure yet which ones to charge with which crimes. He knows they've all been involved in the crime, but he doesn't know to what extent. It happens with gang assaults, or a group shoplifting or several people using a stolen credit card. Who threw the first punch or who actually stole the goods, and who was distracting the clerk, or who knew that the credit card was stolen are typical problems of "a real mess." It takes patience, but with time the facts can be gleaned.

A "cluster," in addition to being a strange term is also a pretty accurate term. It is usually "a real mess" complicated by confusing or incorrect paperwork done by several people. Clusters can be very tedious. The paperwork can be court orders which are impossible to carry out, arrest warrants written for the wrong person or bench warrants with "facts" that are just wrong. The possibilities are unlimited but almost always involve either several people under arrest or a few under arrest and many more in the magistrate's lobby demanding an explanation. Usually, the matter can be sorted out once all the players are separated and listened to individually. That is frequently a luxury the cop on the scene does not have available, which is why it gets brought to the magistrate where a sorting can take place.

The worse thing an officer can come to you with is a "situation," and that's what this officer did. Situations can hurt you. Situations are painful. Situations can leave scars.

The officer had arrested a teenage boy on a war-

rant for rape of a teenage girl. It was not a violent
rape. The boy apparently talked the girl into taking
her clothes off, but when she wanted him to stop, he
didn't. He kept persisting and eventually penetrated
her. A few days later she went to the counselor to
ask him what to do. The reason there was a counsel-
lor was that she and the boy lived in a group home
for mentally retarded young people. Now the officer
had the mentally retarded boy under arrest, charged
with rape, and his father was waiting in the lobby,
hoping to be able to take his son home. That is a
situation.

The father was a retired army officer, and I cannot
imagine the anguish he was going through that night.
I asked the police officer if he had talked to the girl's
parents. He had and said that they seemed to be amazingly understanding. They now had their daughter
home with them. I brought the father into a private
office for a conversation I knew would be very difficult
for both of us.

He was a remarkable man. He told me immediately that whatever I decided to do he would understand, and he realized he was asking for a lot to take
his son home.

"Is your wife not with you?" I asked.

"No, she's at home. She just can't cope with this
yet."

"Do you know the girl's parents?"

"Yes, I've met them a few times." He looked devastated.

"I understand that they are not unsympathetic to
your request."

He smiled sadly and said, "They seemed to be

very nice the few times I've met them."

"I certainly can't send your son back to the home tonight, and I don't like the idea of keeping him in jail either. If I were to allow him to go home with you, do you think you will have any problems with him?"

"No, we've always gotten along well. He's really a nice kid. We had him in the home in the hope that he could eventually be on his own. He does quite well sometimes." A tear glistened down his cheek.

I knew I had to talk to the boy, and it seemed like a good time to excuse myself to do that. This conversation was tearing my heart out. I went into the jail and, as his father had said, he was a nice kid. He was mildly retarded and felt awful about what he had done. He looked at me and said quietly, "I know what I did was wrong, and I'll have to be punished for that." He was in pathetic misery.

I thought, though, that the girl and her parents were probably in even more pain and misery. Lord, what a mess!

I went back to the police officer and asked, "You've talked to her parents. If I let him go with the father, do you have any feel for what their reaction might be?"

He thought about it for a second and said slowly, "I don't think it would upset them. They're aware of the circumstances of the rape." He hesitated and said, "If there is anything such as a gentle rape, sir, this was one."

I eventually released the son to the father. Keeping him in jail was helping no one. It was going to just add more pain to what was already numbing agony. I didn't feel that there was a right or wrong — just sadness.

Chapter 34

Lost In the System

$\mathcal{I}$t is disturbing when the system breaks down completely. On the way in one day I noticed an older man standing outside the jail. He was hard not to notice as he was six feet eight inches tall, weighed about 300 pounds, and was surrounded by three very large, cheap suitcases and other bits and pieces of stuff. He was smiling and wearing a suit and tie.

When I got into the office, I asked what the deal was with him. Other people had noticed him but no one knew what he was doing. It was a busy day, and it was a few hours before I was able to look outside and see if he was still there. He was, and still smiling. I felt I should go ask.

I went out and introduced myself. He was quite pleasant and affable and barely spoke English. I discovered he was German and between his little English and my rudimentary German I gleaned an odd tale.

He lived in West Germany and had decided a month

ago to gather all his things, buy a plane ticket to the United States and find an American family to adopt him. He was sixty-one years old.

After arriving, he decided that the best way to find the right family was to go to Washington D.C. and see the President about it. He understood that the President was a very busy man but, after a month of being told by the White House guards that the President was not going to be able to see him, he ran out of money and was asked to leave by the hotel where he was staying. With no money and no place to go he simply attempted to set up house in the hotel lobby. Eventually, the police were called and, after many attempts to get him to leave, he was arrested for trespassing.

After three weeks in jail, because he was unable to post a $250 bond, the courts appointed him a lawyer who was able to argue that even if his client were eventually to be found guilty of trespass at a trial that was many weeks down the road, he would in all likelihood not be sentenced to more than three weeks for such a nonviolent act, and since he had essentially served his time, he should be released.

As far as his client's somewhat odd behavior and belief that he would eventually be adopted by an American family at the age of sixty one, he had been seen by various court-appointed psychiatrists, who were of the opinion that his client was not a danger to himself or anyone else. Since a mental detention in an institution required such imminent danger and none was apparent, the smiling German was released. The attorney made contact with the German Embassy, which was not interested in getting involved.

So there we stood, outside the jail amidst all this

poor man's possessions. No place to go and not a clue what to do. He couldn't just stand there forever. He didn't even have money to eat.

I considered the fact that there are plenty of Americans in the same situation and what do we do with them? They go to a homeless shelter. A wonderful woman in the office called around and made all the arrangements at a shelter and was even able to get bus tokens for him. We wrote out the directions in English for him to give to the bus driver, since there was a transfer to be made. I loaded him and his stuff in my car and took him to the bus stop. I shook his hand, gave him $10, and wished him well. We told the shelter to be on the lookout for him.

Though homeless shelters, in general, do not have a good reputation, the shelters in the county had always impressed me as well-run places. I had no other ideas, anyway. The only problem was, he never arrived. Whether he changed his mind and perhaps decided to go back to the White House for one more try, or just screwed up the bus transfer, I'll never know. I never heard from him or about him again. I hope he's well and happy somewhere. He was a gentle, nice man.

The angriest I ever was about the system involved a teenage girl with Down's Syndrome who was grabbed between the legs by a pervert at a bus stop. Some good citizens grabbed the creep and held him for the police. When they arrived, the girl was hysterical. The officers determined that the girl lived in a home for people with Down's Syndrome and decided not to arrest the man. They knew him as a neighborhood drunk and were confident that they could pick him up anytime they needed.

They took the girl to the home and explained what had happened. They also explained how to see a magistrate to get a warrant for sexual battery. I was not too happy with the police on this one. I thought they should have arrested the slimeball immediately. As it turned out, they seemed to have had an instinct about the case that I did not. The next day the girl, her parents and the home director showed up at the magistrate's office. The magistrate available happened to be me.

After listening to the director, the girl's parents, and the girl, I had but one reservation. The girl was able to describe well enough to me what had happened, and I saw no problem as far as her being able to testify effectively in court. Before I wrote the warrant, I asked them to go see someone in the commonwealth attorney's office. It would be blindsiding them if the prosecuting attorney did not discover until the day of the trial that the victim suffered from Down's Syndrome.

I did not want anything but the best possible prosecution for this case. Since the charge was a misdemeanor, the prosecuting attorney would not meet the victim until the morning of the trial. There are just too many misdemeanor cases and not enough prosecutors to allow time for extensive pretrial meetings. It is a bad state of affairs, and one that is not improving. We work with it the best we can. I thought that by sending them to talk to a prosecuting attorney first, I was remedying that problem in this case.

They returned about an hour later in a state of shock. The commonwealth attorney's office had refused to prosecute the case. I was flabbergasted. I might have been more shocked than they were. They told me that the prosecutor said the girl would not be able to give strong enough or coherent enough testimony. I sat listening to them in embarrassment. They understood it was not my decision, but were hopeful I could do something. I explained there was no point in writing a warrant if the commonwealth attorney's office refused to prosecute the case. I could only say I would follow up on it and get back with them.

I did and got nowhere with the prosecutor. He repeated many times that she would not be able to testify well enough on the stand for a conviction. I had heard the girl's testimony, and I knew he could get a conviction. He was adamant, and I was adamant. If I couldn't convince him to prosecute, I was sunk. I kept at him, but in the end, I failed. This idiot seemed to want to handle only college-graduate victims.

I told him that he was a disgrace. If the poor girl had been dragged into the woods and raped and killed, would that have made her a more believable victim? It was heartbreaking having to tell her parents that a degenerate pervert was going to get away with abusing their daughter. It was clear to me that there were two despicable characters involved, and one of them wore a three-piece suit.

"They have no lawyers among them,
for they consider them as a sort of people
whose profession is to disguise matters"
— Sir Thomas More,
Utopia: Of Law and Magistrates

Chapter 35

Feliz Navidad

*H*olidays are miserable. On one-day holidays, like St. Patrick's Day, which is even worse than New Year's Eve, everybody seems to go out and get drunk, rowdy, and arrested. Such days may get busy, but not too complicated. Days that the Washington Redskins play and win are in this category, too. Days that they lose are not. Assaults and mean drunks are the order of the day then.

I don't pay too much attention to football, but when I'm working and the home town team is playing, I root for them. A stream of bruised and obnoxious drunks all evening gets pretty depressing. A common belief is sweet, loving, docile little wives get beaten whenever the home team loses. It's really not so. The reality is that often the wives are as drunk and obnoxious as their husbands.

The longer holidays such as Thanksgiving or Christmas — the family holidays — are the worst.

Brothers, sisters, aunts, uncles, inlaws and outlaws who see each other once or twice a year, and like it that way, are thrown together to give thanks, or presents, and are expected to act as if they enjoy getting together. The charade lasts for a day or two, and then cracks in the façade begin to develop.

Discussions about politics, or sports or each other's children after a few days in close confines easily slide into arguments, screaming matches and fistfights. Somebody calls the cops and, since it's family, the cops have to call more cops because the "family" tells the cops to butt out when they arrive, even though there's a boxing match going on in the living room. It gets pretty messy, and several times during these "family" holidays I have to arbitrate disputes that have been festering for years. They take a lot of time, too, because everyone wants to tell their side of the story starting with 1946 or so. The usual outcome is everybody goes away, those not locked up that is, unhappy with me, themselves, and each other.

Christmas is the worst. There is an increase in the number of mental-detention orders is because of Christmas depression so many people go through. Add to that the huge surge in shoplifting arrests, and one can see why magistrates can be somewhat subdued about celebrating a Merry Christmas.

When you really get down to it, Christmas is miserable. Secretly, most people agree. They think it is a sacrilege to admit it, but I have lost count of the number of people who have told me how much they dread the Christmas holidays — not the people who are alone during the holidays, but those with all the family obligations. When I am refereeing these family blowouts, a common lament I hear is that the problems are the same ones that have been unresolved for years. Resentment and animosity that bubble quietly under the surface all year long are amplified when the extended family has to be in close proximity for a few days.

After several years of listening to these family tribulations, I'm here to tell you, if you think your family is screwed up, don't feel like the Lone Ranger. You've got plenty of company, and if you've never been to see a magistrate, yours is probably not as screwed up as many.

Christmas Eve used to be a special time to be home with family. Perhaps because Christmas has become so secularized, it is now more of a time to go visiting to toast the occasion. I discovered it is also becoming a tradition in the Hispanic community, as well.

The police responded to a loud party and, regrettably, it had gotten out of hand. There were a number of intoxicated people in the courtyard of the apartment complex. Some were becoming unruly, and, reluctantly, the police made several arrests. Nobody wants to be the Christmas Grinch, but many of the neighbors were complaining about the drinking and noise.

I was scheduled to work that Christmas Day, and arrived at 7:00 a.m., expecting a very slow, easy day. After all, who gets arrested Christmas Eve or Day? My surprise was total when I walked into the office and saw two very tired, worn out magistrates, and an overwhelming stack of arrest warrants. Not the traditional Kodak Christmas moment. One looked at me wearily and sighed, "We just put in the last drunk ten minutes ago. It was nonstop all night long. There's forty that need to be released when they sober up. We were barely keeping up with the drunk Anglos when the police brought in about twenty people from some Hispanic party. It went downhill from there. Good luck getting it sorted out. A bunch of them were so drunk when they came in they didn't know their names. I never wrote so many John Doe and Juan Doe warrants in my life."

As they both shuffled toward the door, I wished them an admittedly weak, "Merry Christmas."

I was not a happy magistrate. Christmas morning and I was facing the prospect of several hours of releasing smelly, hungover drunks and trying to sort out several Juan Does and John Does from one another. As I went through the pile of warrants, I saw there was one action I needed to take first. I called the jail and said, "I see three drunks you've got by the name of Jesus. On this, of all days, we need to release them immediately. So anybody by the name of Jesus who can walk and sign his release papers, bring 'em over."

That improved my spirits some. At least I had a plan. Next in keeping with that theme I released all the Josephs and Joses. I then asked if any Marys or Marias had been brought in. It was nice that there were none. Next I asked for the Peters and Pedros and Johns and Juans, working through the Apostles.

After the Apostles and Disciples were out, I was left with John and Juan Does. As they sobered up and began giving their names, or their families showed up and supplied them, the winnowing process continued. That got a little tedious, but by mid-morning I was done, having in the process reunited many wayward husbands and fathers with their worried, now greatly relieved families, who had come down to the jail on

Christmas morning, hoping to get Papa out and spruced up in time for Christmas services.

Most of the wives who showed up started off with a chagrined, "Merry Christmas. I think you have my husband in jail." The Spanish-speaking wives similarly greeted me with, "*Feliz Navidad*," and then looked at me expectantly. I knew the nontraditional translation — "Merry Christmas. Is my husband in your jail?

"There is in all men a demand for the superlative, so much so that the poor devil who has no other way of reaching it attains it by getting drunk."
— Oliver Wendell Holmes

Chapter 36

DWI – Too Drunk to Walk

I have become very intolerant of drunk drivers. It is the height of arrogance to drink too much and then get into a car and wantonly menace every one else on the road with death and injury. It will continue to be a deadly situation until the courts get serious about it and start giving people *real* jail time for a DWI offense. All the public relations ploys legislators and judges are pulling to convince the public they are doing something are just that: dishonest legerdemains that accomplish nothing. After twelve years as a magistrate, I still do not know why the charade. Why do we not give DWI violators serious jail time? I do not understand why perpetrators of a crime that kills tens of thousands of innocent victims a year get a very, very slight tap on the wrist and an admonition to try real hard not to do it again. It infuriates me and frustrates me.

However, having said that, even I who hate DWI's

and have written probably over 3,000 DWI arrest warrants, have to admit to a few occasions when I had to laugh. Only three out of three thousand, though, does give you an idea of how little levity comes from DWI cases.

The police responded to a call one night at 2:00 a.m. of a burglary in progress. A woman was on the phone reporting that her husband was in a fight with a burglar in their garage. Such a call gets the adrenalin in the police really flowing and cops responded from all directions at a high rate of speed. There is a saying in the police department, "Make a cop come, call 911."

In a very few moments, the house was besieged by eager, excited cops, ready to do battle. Sure enough, there was a fist fight in the garage between two men. The garage door was open, and a sea of cops swarmed in, each officer wanting to be first to land a blow. It was over in a second. Any taxpaying homeowner would have been thrilled to see his tax dollars at work. The cavalry arrived — big time.

The burglar turned out to be a drunk driver who had mistaken the open garage as his own garage, and he had pulled right in. When the police had peeled him off the garage floor, he was still screaming that he had been attacked in his own garage by some crazed madman. In fact, the madman was the homeowner, who had heard noises in his garage and, when he had gone to investigate, had been attacked by the drunk who thought he, in turn, was being attacked by a maniac.

The wife had identified the rightful homeowner to the police as they surged in. When the drunk was taken off to jail, he was still protesting that it was his house. Had he lived on the same street, maybe such a mistake could be understood. Instead, incredibly, he had missed his own garage by ten miles. I had to laugh, listening to the drunk's protestations about being arrested. Still, it's scary, someone that drunk driving a car.

On another night, an officer was sitting at a traffic light when a car coming through the intersection went out of control and ended up in the median. It rained heavily earlier in the day, and when the car hit the median area, a huge eruption of water went up. When visible again it was axle deep in mud with the engine roaring, but going nowhere. The officer shook her head, sighed, and pulled up a few lengths behind the car, turning on her emergency lights. Since the wheels were still spinning and throwing mud, the officer walked a wide detour and came up from the driver's side of the stuck car, its engine still roaring.

As she approached, she saw the driver anxiously looking in his rear view mirror at the flashing red-and-blue lights on his tail, then trying to peer through the windshield, which was covered with muck. He turned on the windshield wipers, which did clear the mess, looked in the mirror again, and floored it as he hunched over the steering wheel in his best NASCAR imitation.

Understandably not wanting to get too near this idiot, the officer just waited and watched developments. The car sank deeper into the mud as the dope tried to shake his pursuer. After a few moments of this, our obviously drunk speedster decided that if he could not shake the cops at 90 m.p.h., he would slow down to around 40 m.p.h. and settle in for a long run for the border.

Since the car was now buried so deep in the mud that it wasn't throwing any debris, and the engine was down to a steady roar instead of a scream, the officer ventured to the side of the car and began pounding on the door with her flashlight. The drunk made a few annoyed, unfocused glances in her direction and ignored her. Maybe he thought the noise was various road signs and other road hazards he was sweeping aside as he rampaged down the highway.

She leaned over and shined her flashlight through the windshield and noticed that he would focus on the light and steer away from it. If she held it farther over to the right he would steer and lean left. Enough was enough. The noise was getting on her nerves and so was this idiot, so she stepped back a few feet, pulled her night stick, and began pounding on the roof of the car with such force that the drunk could not ignore her.

Still driving, he rolled down his window and was greeted by a very irate face a few inches from his that screamed, "Pull this piece of s--t over right now!"

It was more than his booze soddened mind could handle. He glanced down at his speedometer (40 m.p.h.) and then at the rearview mirror and the flashing blue-and-red lights and then back at the cop in his window. He was the definition of astonishment.

"Yes, ma'am, anything you say, ma'am," he stammered in amazement as he took his foot off the pedal and steered for the side of the road. When the officer brought the drunk before me, he was still mesmerized by her. He'd seen Wonder Woman on television, but he was too drunk, dazed, and amazed to understand any of the testimony. He did have one question as she led him off to jail, "How come I was the one you pulled over?"

One evening the police brought in a nineteen-year-old DWI. His breath test showed him to be over the limit, but just barely. He was a very pleasant young man and very polite. I couldn't release him once the alcohol was gone, because he was from Connecticut and was just visiting. I noticed on the police report that his car had Virginia tags.

"How is it you are from Connecticut but your car has Virginia tags?" I asked.

He looked embarrassed as he answered, "I used to live here, and I'm staying with our old next door neighbor, and it's his car."

"He'll be real happy to find out his car has been towed and impounded tonight," I noted.

The officer volunteered, "Actually, sir, it wasn't. The young lady with him is the daughter of the neighbor. She's eighteen and hadn't had anything to drink, so she drove the car home."

"That's fortunate," I said. "Too bad you didn't let her drive in the first place."

He shook his head woefully and agreed. "Too late now, sir."

"Well, I'll have to think about what to do with you. You go with the jailor, and I'll let you know how I'm going to release you."

An hour later, I still hadn't decided what to do with the kid, when a tall solidly built man arrived at the public's window with a pretty, but worried-looking young girl with him. The neighbor had arrived. He introduced himself and said, "My daughter here came home and told me her date got arrested for DWI, and I understand you're holding him."

"Yes, that's right, and I'm not sure what to do with him."

He looked at me and said, "That makes two of us. I feel like letting him stay here and rot. I mean, he comes down to visit and I loan him my car and allow him to take my daughter out and the little bastard goes out with her and gets drunk."

His daughter, standing behind him, looked like she was having the absolute worst day of her life. Her father wasn't so much mad as obviously deeply disappointed. Daughter was in agony.

As I watched her, he followed my look. She was so woebegone, I saw his expression begin to soften. "Well, he always was a pretty good kid, and his father and I are in the Marines. What's the procedure here?"

I explained that if he were to sign for him, guaranteeing his appearance in court, I would release the kid to his custody. I told him that the court would expect $500 from him if the young man missed court. Daughter looked pained.

"Hmm," from father. He didn't look too convinced as he considered that. Then slowly his face changed as a new line of thought developed. "Say, if I sign for him does he come out through this lobby?"

"Yes."

"There's no other way out?"

"No."

Daughter began to look a little panicked.

"If I sign for him, will you release him right now, while I wait?"

"Yes. It's a different twist, but I'll give him early release for not-so-good behavior."

He began to grind a fist into his palm as he considered. "I think that's what I'd like to do," he said as a slow smile came on his face.

Daughter looked on the verge of fainting. I thought my idea an excellent one. I asked for his identification and noted that he was a Marine Corps colonel. If I had thought the colonel was actually going to physically assault the kid, I wouldn't have released him. But somehow I knew that, even though it was going to go pretty hard for him, he was in no real physical danger. He had been a great deal more at risk while driving drunk. I knew he was facing some tough going, though, deservedly so.

When they brought him for release, I said, "There's good news and there's bad news. The good news is you're getting out." He looked relieved at that. "The bad news is that the colonel is waiting in the lobby for you." At that the kid turned ashen.

"Is there another way out?" he asked.

"No."

"Do I have to go?"

"Yes."

He took a couple of hard swallows, and his signature was a little unsteady. As he was escorted toward the door by the jailors, I heard one of them say to him in response to his explanations, "Jeez, kid, her old man, huh? And his car? And a Marine? Whew! Glad I don't have to go out there."

"When you have no basis for an argument,
abuse the plaintiff"
— Cicero

Chapter 37

What's In a Name?

The man had more aliases, social security numbers, and dates of birth than a Sing-Sing cell block. The police had been interviewing the guy for hours after he had been caught trying to use a stolen credit card at a department store. It was one of many they found on him. He was surprisingly cooperative when apprehended and had helpfully given the police his name, address, and date of birth with no hassle.

The problem began when that name came back as wanted for grand larceny. Oops. Well, maybe that wasn't him after all.

"Just funnin', officers," smiled our thief. "This is my real name." Another call to the station for a record check.

"Gee, that name came back wanted too, huh — for burglary? Imagine that."

Things were getting a mite bit uncomfortable. Such things do not amuse the police.

"Look," said the detective. "We got you cold for stolen credit card. How about quit screwin' around and just give up your real name so we can all go home?"

"We?" said John Doe, hopefully.

"Just a figure of speech," said the detective. "And besides, you do have a home tonight. You may not like the decor or your roommates, but we think it's a pretty respectable jail. You don't have to worry about your virginity."

"Thanks for those comforting words, detective."

"How about think real hard who you are. The magistrate is gonna knock your brains out with a high bond if we have to tell him we don't know and you can't remember."

This went on for two hours and seven different names. The guy wasn't combative, and he didn't even have a chip on his shoulder. But damned if he could get his name right. By the time he was brought to me, he had reached a certain rapprochement with the police. Everybody was pretty much at ease.

"Mr. Jasper, I bring before you Mr. John Doe. Mr. Doe has been decent enough but he has two big problems. He can't seem to remember his name, and he has very definitely been hanging out with the wrong crowd. I kind of doubt you're going to have much success helping him with his memory lapse. He's been made aware of the problem that creates with such fair-minded magistrates as yourself when you consider his bond. The amusing thing about the seven different names our chum here has given us is every single one is wanted and had outstanding warrants. We're pretty sure he's just using his buddies' names. They're real names, he's not making them up. Doesn't say much for his choice of friends, does it? When number seven showed up wanted for murder, he kind of decided maybe he was getting out of the name game."

Mr. John Doe was smiling pleasantly at me.

"Mr. Doe, let's be realistic about this. I've been doing this job for twelve years, and you get a feel for things in twelve years. I know you've been arrested before. Everybody knows you've been arrested before, even if we don't know who you are. Eventually, the police will figure that out. It's only a matter of time, and I can't even consider you for bail if I don't have a clue as to your identity. So let's be adult about this, quit the charade and give us your real name."

He looked at me earnestly and said, "It must be some problem with the computers. I'm who I say I am."

"Seven different times?" I asked

"It doesn't make sense to me, either, Mr. Magistrate."

I looked at the detectives. "Ducks and weaves a lot, I see."

"He's been that way from the start, sir."

"I'm holding you without bond, Mr. Doe. I really have no other choice. If a man's seven closest friends are all wanted then I have to assume you are, too."

"You don't know that's true, Mr. Magistrate."

"So, how about your name and let's see?"

"You have my name."

"Could be, but we don't know which of the seven it is. Are you Sneezy, or Grumpy or Dopey — hey, you've haven't done anything bad to Snow White have you?"

As the jailors took him away we began diligently working on naming the rest of the Dwarves.

"Why should there not be a patient confidence
in the ultimate justice of the people?
Is there any better or equal hope in the world?"
— Abraham Lincoln

Chapter 38

Arrogance On the Bench

Sometimes the judicial system gets so stupid, I seriously consider resigning just because I don't want to be associated with such an illogical, impersonal, and arrogant operation. Millions are spent studying problems in the criminal justice system. Seminars are held at fancy resorts to admire the beautifully packaged reports which reach conclusions incomprehensible even to the people who wrote them. Some even attempt to conclude there are no problems.

Most of the people are misguided, if well intentioned. Others are blatantly attempting to justify a particular agenda they are pushing. Few address the very real problem of the public losing faith in the system. It's not that complicated. All one need do is look at the asinine rulings handed down from the benches and, with a little bit of thought, it's crystal clear why people think judges have lost their minds.

A magistrate, six months ago, wrote arrest warrants for abduction and malicious wounding against a career criminal who had one murder in the seventies another in the eighties and numerous assaults and woundings while in prison. No doubt he had been released from prison early because of credit for "good behavior." The fact that he was out at all is bad enough, but it gets worse. Does it ever get worse.

When in front of the magistrate, the thug said to the arresting officer, who was a female, "When I get out, bitch, be looking over your shoulder. I've killed before, and I'm gonna kill again. You know it don't bother me."

A woman was the victim of his abduction and malicious wounding. This was a homicidal maniac who hated women and was a real threat. His latest victim was still in the hospital. The magistrate held him without bond. Made sense to me.

The next morning at arraignment, the judge set a bond of $1 million. Why he was allowed any bond at all is a wonder. Eventually, he got a court-appointed attorney who, with God knows what kind of irresponsible, self deluding justification, convinced another judge to reduce the bond to $100,000. Obviously, it wasn't the attorney's or the judge's daughter who had been kidnapped and cut up by that psychopath.

What happened next and why is unclear, because afterward everybody who might have been involved suffered a type of amnesia that seems to be peculiar to the court system. The $100,000 bond was appealed to circuit court and a judge there, incredibly, reduced the bond to $10,000. Two prior murders and several assaults!

After a few more weeks in jail, a true obscenity occurred when another judge let the psychopath free without having to post any bond whatsoever. That judge, to this day, has been unavailable for comment. Surprising to no one, except probably the judges, the victim (finally out of the hospital) disappeared. At the trial, the charges were dismissed because there was no victim to testify. She has not been heard of since.

None of the above would have come to my attention, except for the fact that two months after the charges were dismissed, the psychopath was brought in by the police for yet another murder of another woman that he had committed that day. It was only then that I learned of his earlier release and the subsequent dismissal of the charges. At arraignment on the new murder charge, the judge was very concerned that this three- or four-time killer was apprised of all his civil and constitutional rights. I thought he was going to ask him if he had enough pillows in his cell too. At least he didn't release him. That will be later, I presume.

All too many judges have an arrogance that is breathtaking in its boldness. One judge refused to hear further testimony in a general district court case because she had a dental appointment and was not going to be late. The arrogance here was that she announced it in open court before several dozen amazed observers. This same judge did the same thing several months later but that time for a P.T.A. meeting.

Most general district judges are underworked and overpaid. Magistrates all too often must hear mental detentions which are supposed to be done by judges when the courts are open. It has happened that, even though court was open, not even one general district judge could be found in the courthouse. Even though the offices are open until 4:00 p.m., finding a general district judge after 2:00 p.m. is always a problem. Sometimes, even during the trials themselves, general district judges are absent. On one occasion a judge gave the prosecution a ten-minute recess. An hour and a half later, he returned. Where had he been? At a shopping mall two miles away.

Another judge, who was universally known as Rocket J. Squirrel, dismissed every traffic case a state trooper had for court that day. He refused to hear the trooper's testimony about any of the cases. Rocket J. was upset because the trooper had towed a woman's car who had been driving on a suspended license; something the trooper was required to do. Why? Only Rocket J. might know.

One evening, a lady came to me whose husband had been arrested that night for assaulting her. He had a history of assaulting her, and she was very much afraid of what he might do to her if he were to be released. A few days before I had seen photographs of some awful wounds inflicted on a woman after her husband got out of jail, came home, and beat her into a coma with a hammer. The concerns the woman before me was expressing were legitimate and real. I assured her I would not release him, and that he would have to go to an arraignment in the morning before a domestic-relations-court judge.

General district court judges, with all of their

bizarre rulings, are models of sagacity, wisdom, and decorum compared to domestic court judges. I didn't share my thoughts about that with the lady. Knowing that at arraignment all sorts of odd rulings can be handed down, I urged her to be there so that she could tell the judge about her fears for her safety if her husband were to be released. She was very thankful and assured me she would be there.

She came back to me the next afternoon in tears. Her husband was at home laughing at her, drinking and throwing the empty beer cans down the stairs at her. She calmed down enough to tell me the story.

I had told her to be at the arraignment at 9:00 a.m. She had arrived early, at 8:40 a.m., not wanting to be late. To her horror, she discovered that it was over. The arraignment times had been changed to 8:30 a.m. several weeks before by the judges, and no one had bothered to tell the magistrates, who are the ones solely responsible for sending people to arraignments. The judge had ordered the release of the husband, as they very often do.

Not wanting to get the hell beat out of her, she pleaded to talk to the judge. She was so persistent that she managed to get to see him, which is no mean feat in itself. She explained how she had arrived early because the magistrate had emphasized how important it was to be at the arraignment. She begged him to not release her husband. She had done everything the magistrate told her to do. How was she to know anything was wrong? The judge was unimpressed.

I had explained to her the night before about the possibility of getting a protective order from the judge in case her husband did get released. A protective order would have helped to make sure he would not be allowed to return to the house before the trial date. When the judge told her he was going to release the husband with the very odd restriction that he was to confine himself only to the upstairs of the house, she asked if he would consider her petition for a protective order. He flatly refused, telling her that her chance for that had been at the arraignment, which she had missed. The fact that she had done exactly what I told her to do meant nothing to him. Once again, the court won out over common sense. Sad to say, it is not that unusual.

Resigned to her fate, she went home hoping to make the best of a bad situation. It was then that she found her husband already there, drinking and laughing and threatening her. She fled the house and not knowing what else to, came to see me again. It was remarkable that she would talk to me, since she had no reason to think I would care any more than the judge or that I wasn't the incompetent. The poor woman was desperate, though.

I could only tell her that if her husband began threatening to beat her, she should call 911 and get the police over there. She didn't have to wait to get hurt before calling. It would be too late if she did that. I was almost as disheartened as she was when she left. This woman literally put her life into the hands of the court. In return, the court refused to listen and had treated her as an irritant. At probably the most desperate, vulnerable time of her life, the judicial system not only failed to help, but actually increased her risk of serious injury. That is a travesty of justice.

Chapter 39

A Losing Battle

I don't really want to conclude on a down note. But it's very difficult not to if I'm to be honest. The judicial system in this country has huge problems and one of the most intractable ones is that those in the system, and thus part of the problem, refuse to see it. The biggest disappointment, and the most surprising one to me, has been the realization that the best and the brightest are not staying in the legal profession.

I should perhaps qualify that with the observation that my view of the legal profession has been of the criminal side, and I recognize that criminal law is but one part of the complex legal equation. Still, the judges who are drawn from all specialties and supposedly the cream at the top are universally, with some notable exceptions, dull, unimaginative, and arrogant. It is critical to understand that the criminal-justice system cannot work if it does not have the support of the people. That is a very elementary principle that all too many people in that system have either forgotten, or worse, realize but choose to ignore.

The good nature and patience of the American people is almost limitless. The courts, sad to say, have disgracefully relied on that and have intentionally and cynically abused the trust placed in them for far too long. When they should be ashamed, the courts are instead condescending and patronizing. At this moment in 1998, the U.S. legal system is in real danger of becoming impotent.

The quality of life in America has inarguably dropped. There is blame enough to go around to be sure. But the criminal- and civil-justice systems have done more than their share in contributing to that drop. Carefree strolls in our parks in the evening, leisurely walks home from school and pleasant hellos to strangers are a thing of the past. Crooks and shysters have not missed the green light given by lenient sentencing and astounding judgments.

Multimillion-dollar awards to dumb people for doing stupid things like spilling hot coffee in their laps have poisoned the legal well. Crime victims routinely being treated as an annoyance by the courts, while the criminals are indulged and pampered, has become commonplace. Reform is needed — badly.

There is a small glimmer of hope that it is starting. Unfortunately, the reform has had to start from outside. That is not a good situation. When the people in the system itself are the problem, change imposed from the outside is resented and resisted. The judges and lawyers will fight reform because of their rigidity in thinking and arrogance of attitude.

I am sorry to say that I see very little change in that attitude. I would hope that instead of circling the wagons, prominent jurists and leading attorneys would bow to the innate wisdom of the people and become part of a dialogue. I am not optimistic that will happen.

I will continue to do my small part. Yes, it is frustrating, maddening and, at times, almost unen- durable. If I am affected that way as a magistrate, then what must it be for those looking to the system for help? All too often a nightmare, I'm afraid.

I will certainly never, from the basement of the jail, be able to effect meaningful changes in the sys- tem. Still, if I can help those who come for help, lessen the burden of those in need and, perhaps, get a few poor souls back on the right path, I'll stick with it.

About the Author

WENDELL MOORE, PHOTOGRAPHER

John Jasper

After graduating from college with a degree in business and history, John Jasper served a two-and-a-half-year hitch in the Army before moving on to an unusual assortment of jobs around the country for the next three years. Guarding a candy factory, manning a first aid station at a steel mill, and making skis in Colorado preceded his return home to Virginia to begin a career in business management.

After a successful but uneventful decade in the business world, he was appointed a magistrate in 1985. Fourteen years and thousands of cases later, he still finds that the next case is never predictable. He lives with his wife Christine and their beagle Willie in an old farmhouse, beside a stream, at the end of a dirt road.